AF479332

Long ago, in the distant past,
all the animals that are now in Australia
lived in another land beyond the sea;
they were at that time in human form.
One day they met together and decided
to set out in a canoe in order to find
better hunting grounds over the sea.

Dreaming Story from the Thurrawal People of New South Wales

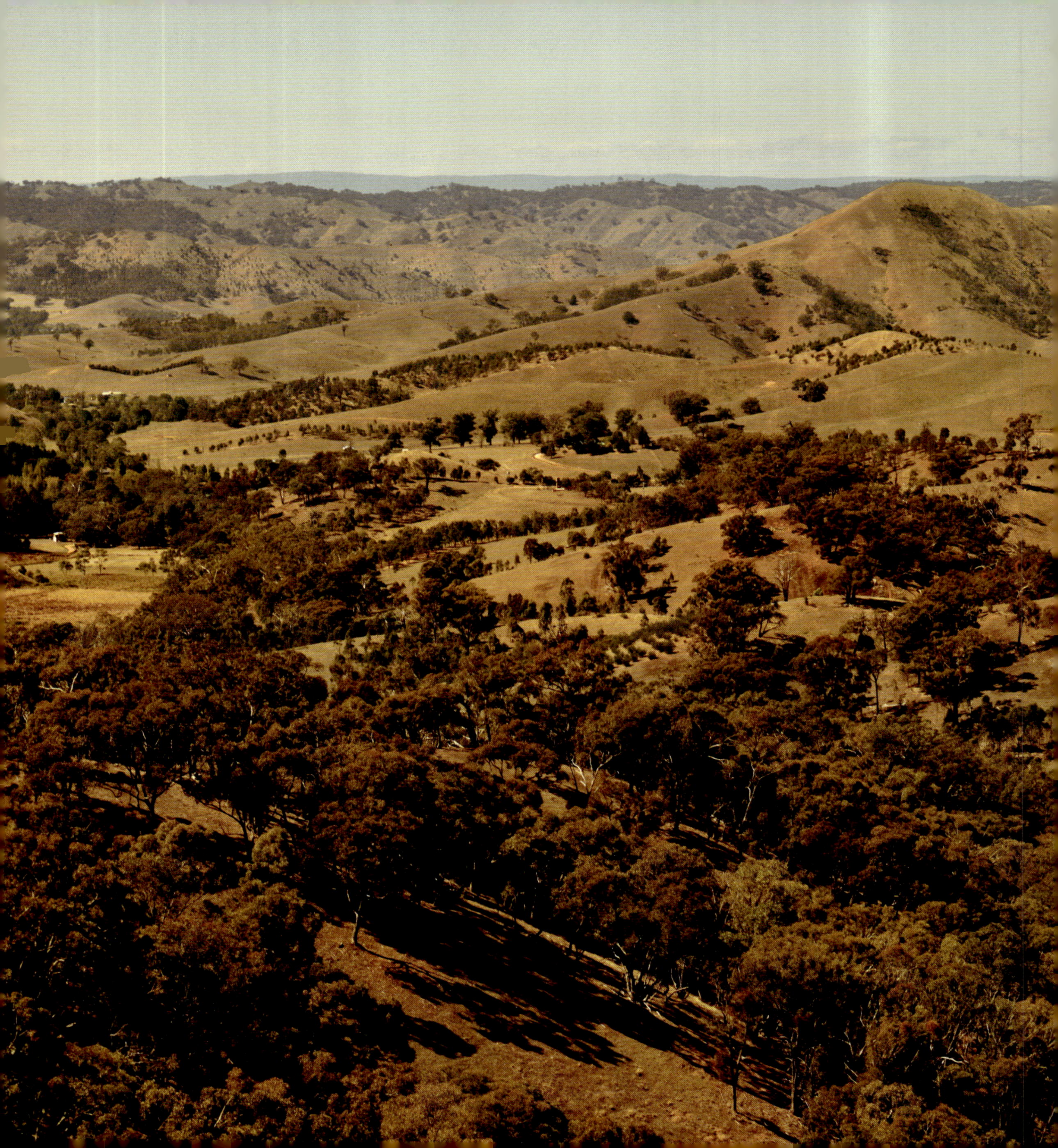

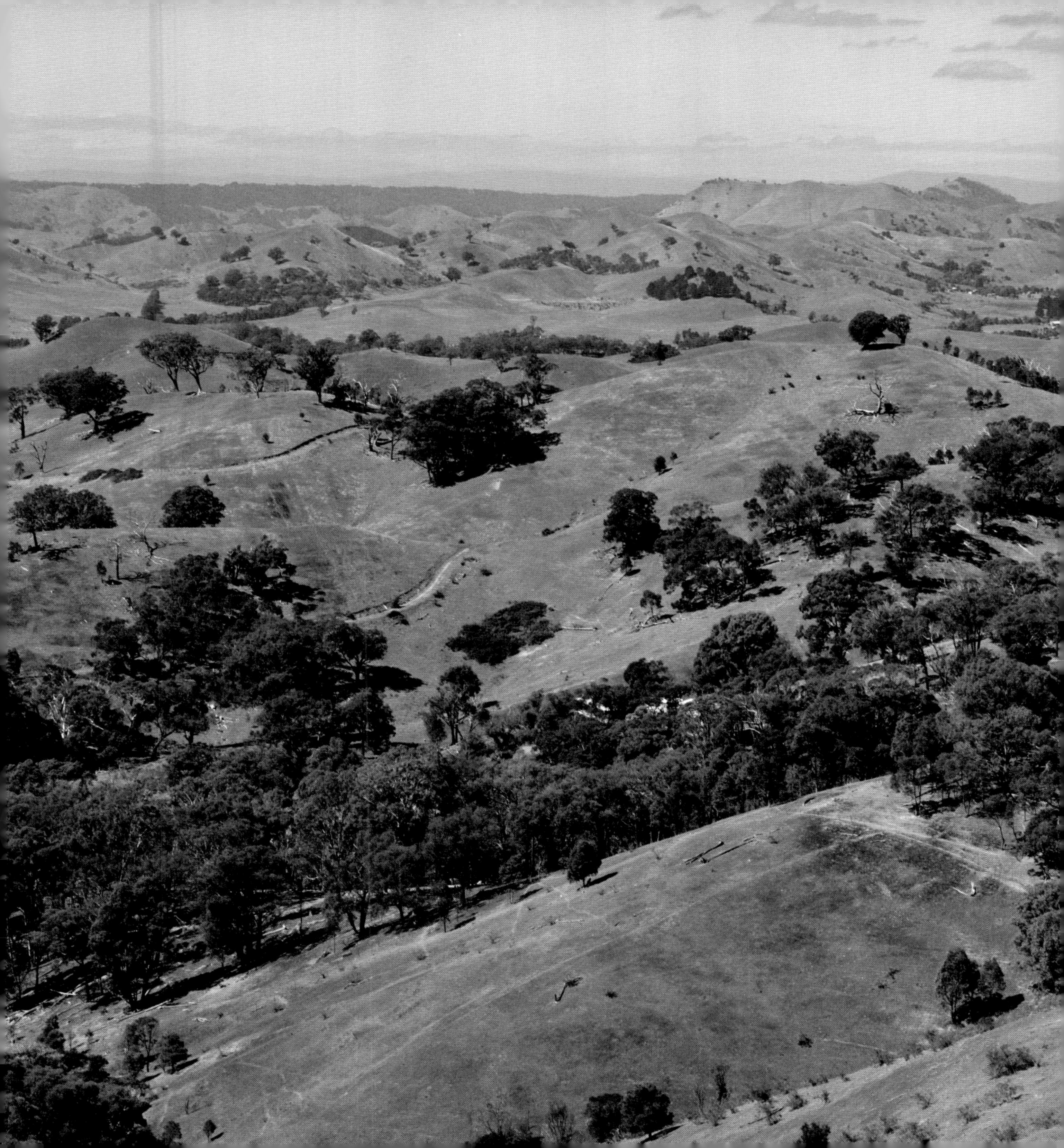

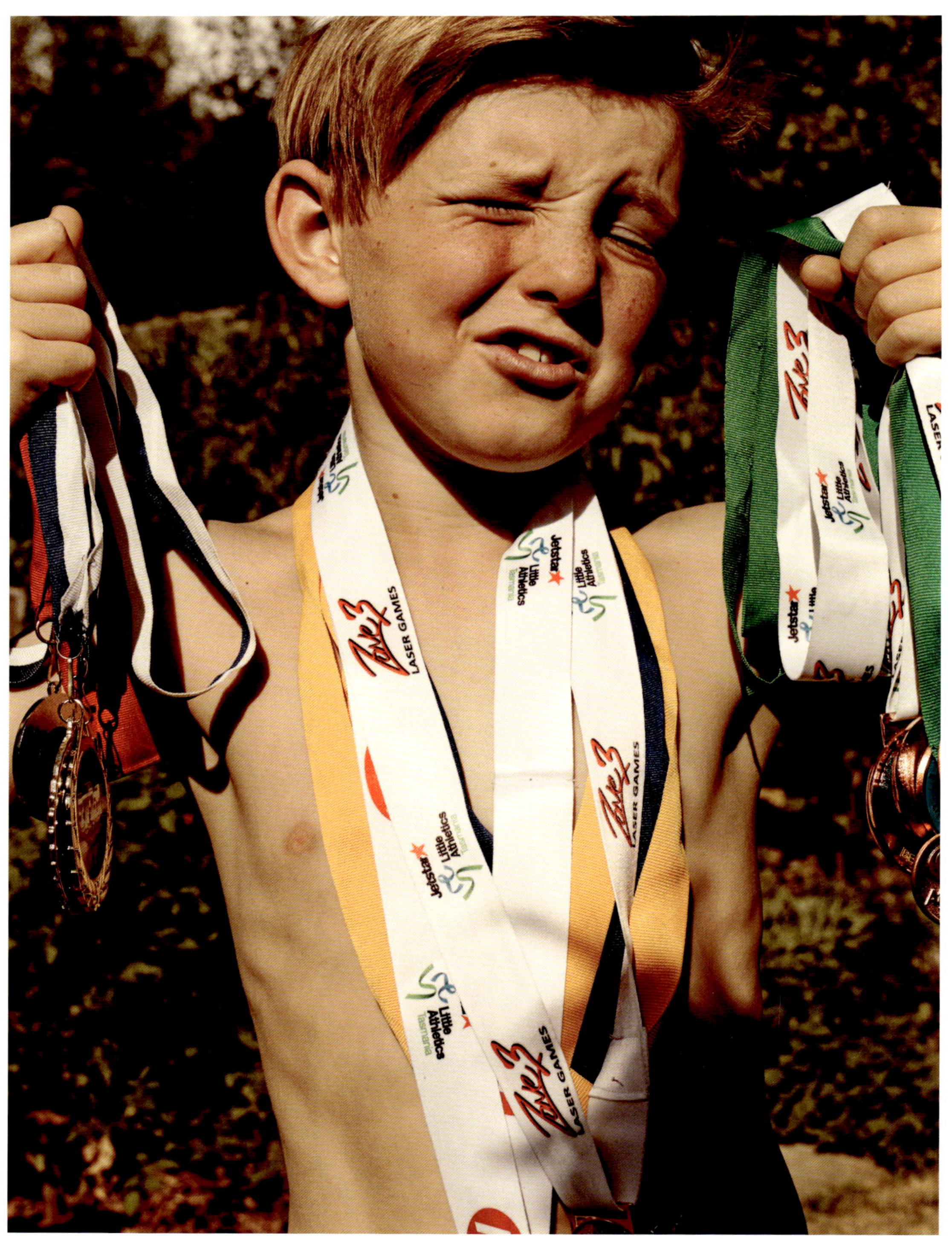

Jesse. Mum's backyard

A
Picture Book
Of
Down Under

Simon Eeles

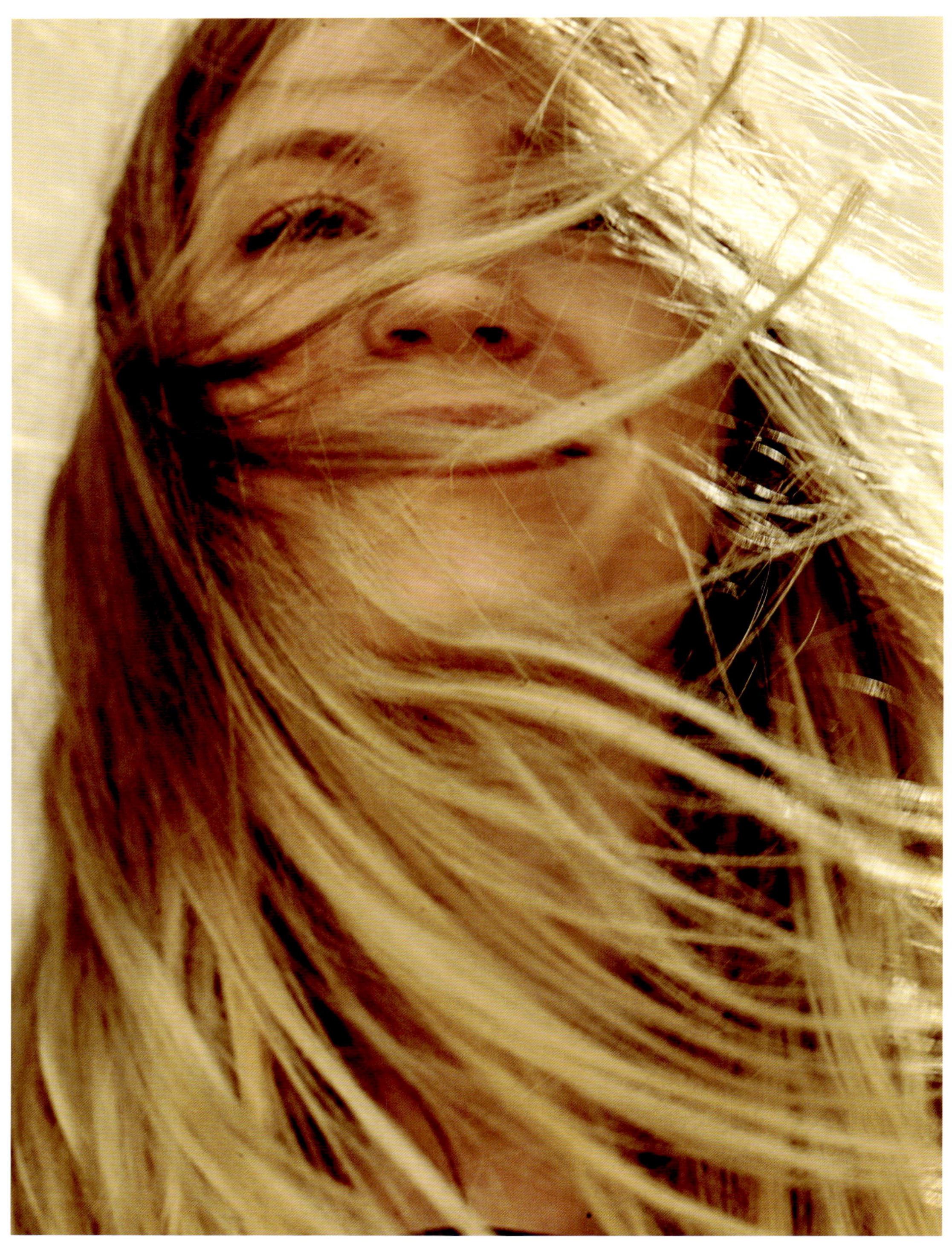

Pearl. Moonee Ponds

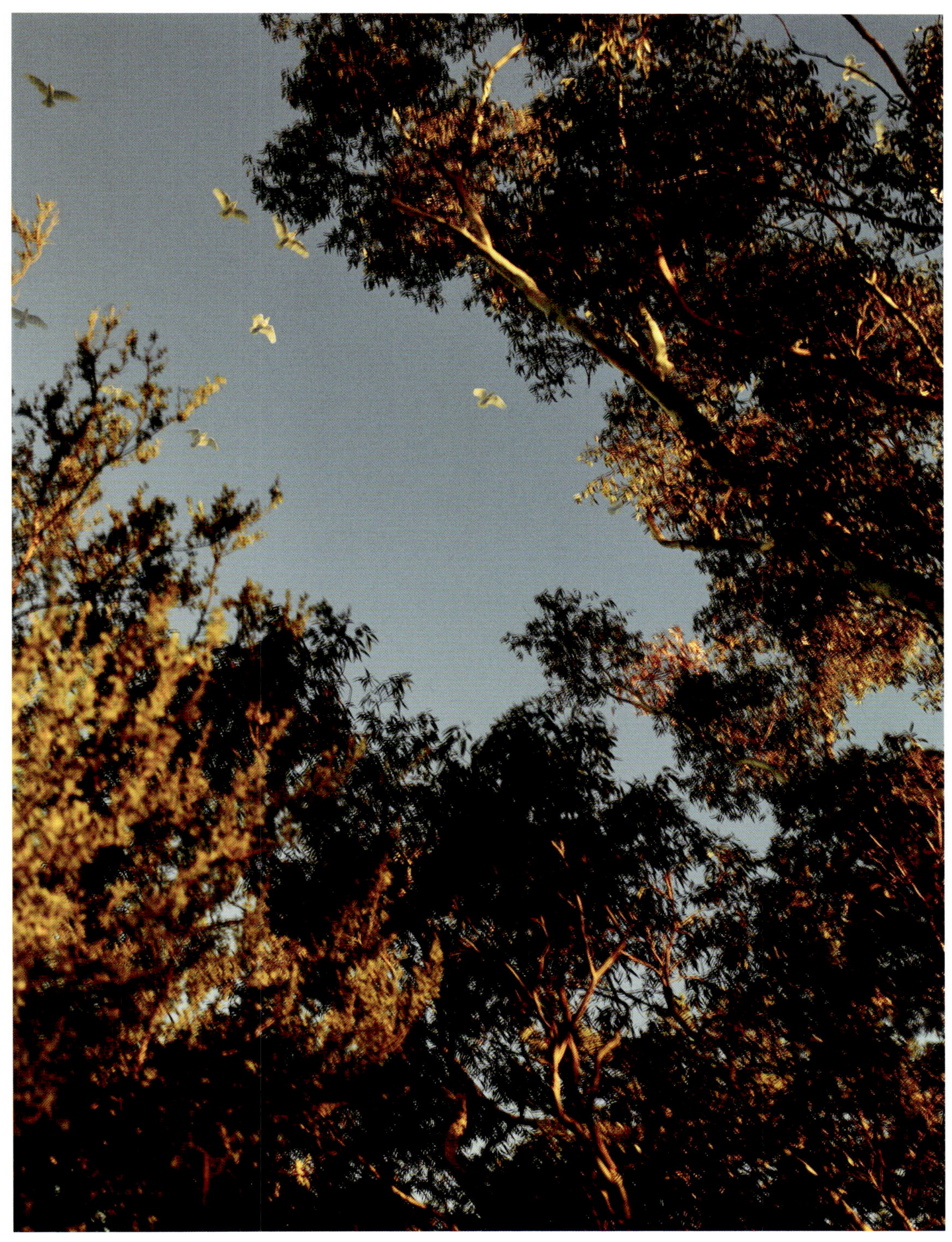

Cockatoo. Mentone

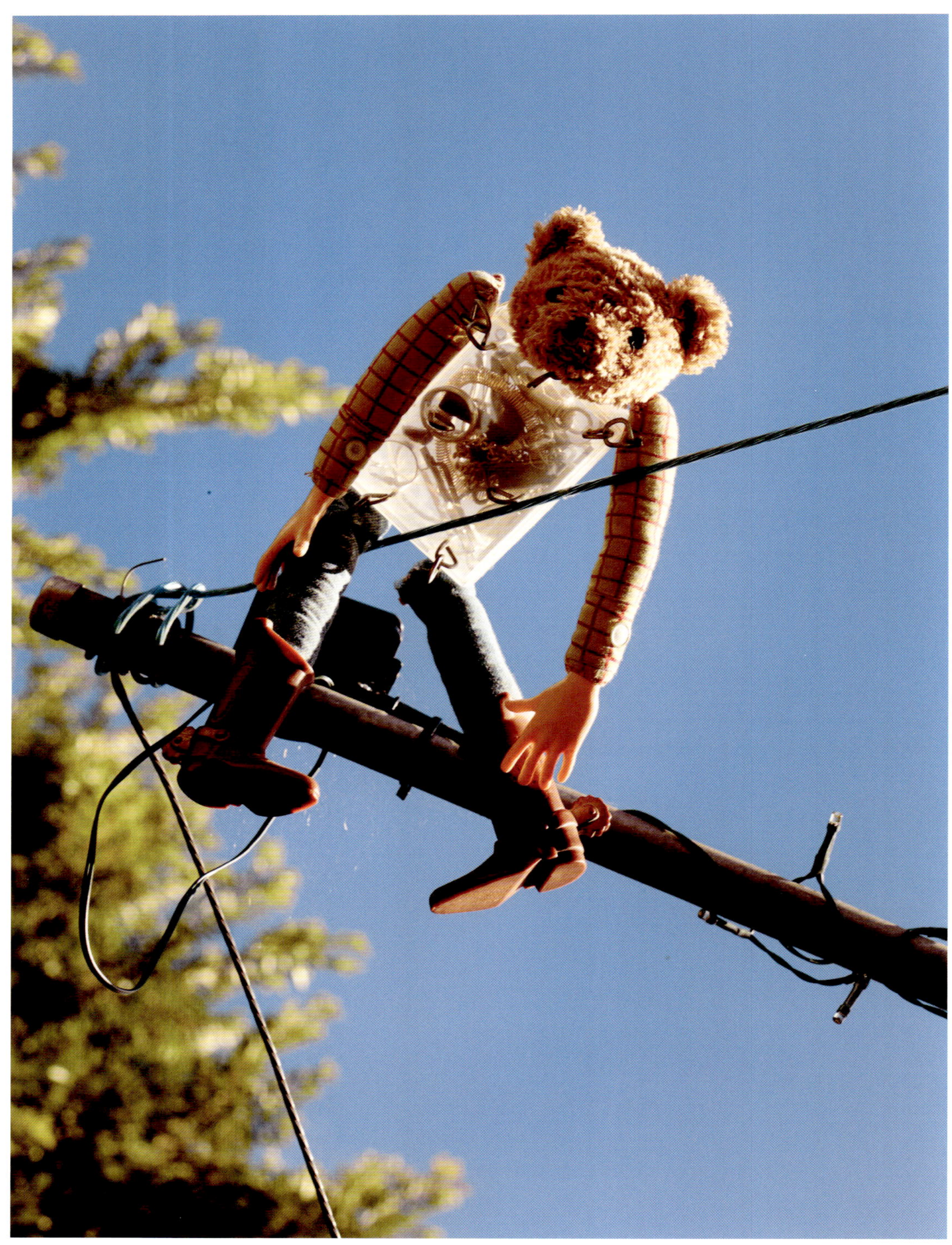

Mr Toolbox. Mum's backyard

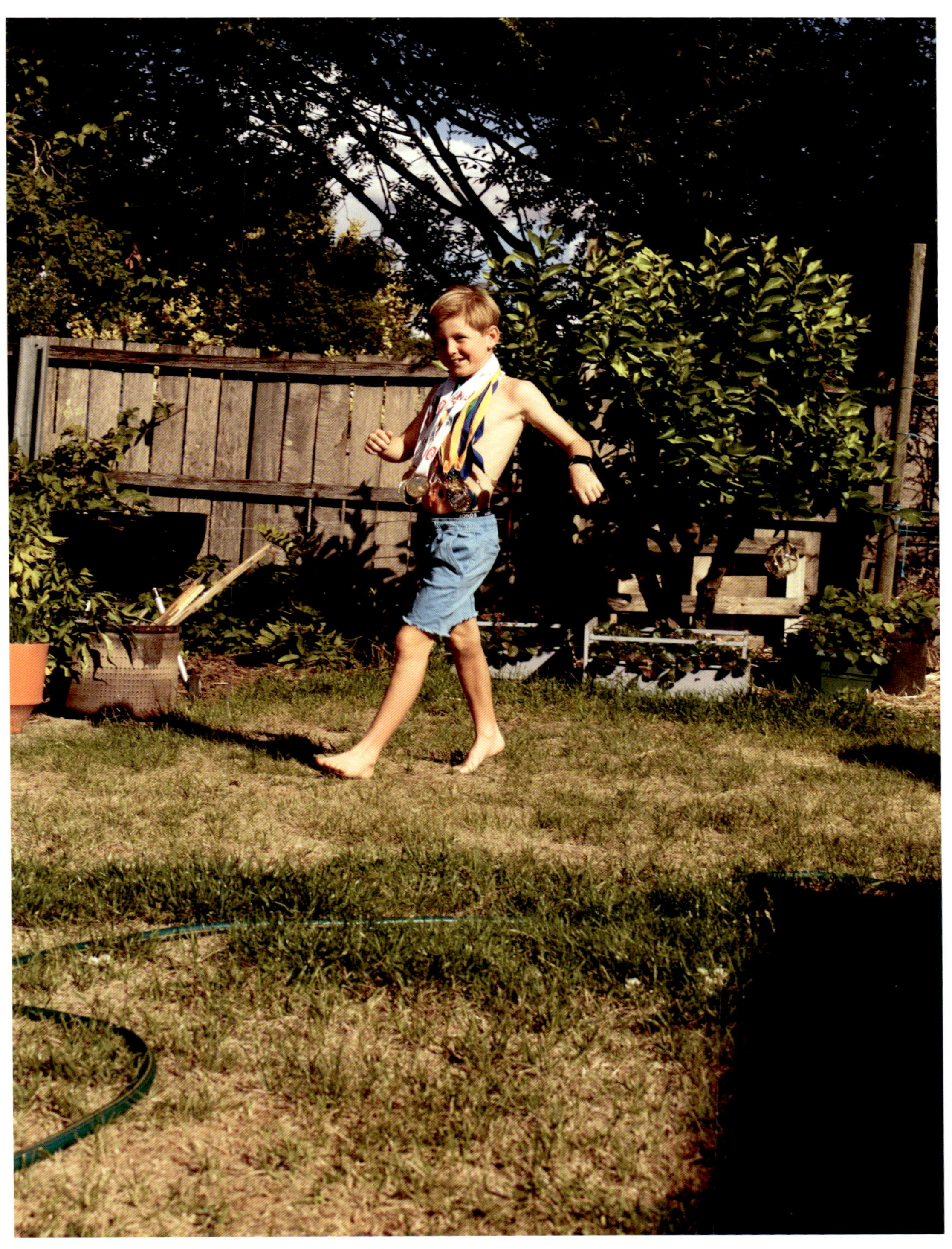

Jesse. Mum's backyard

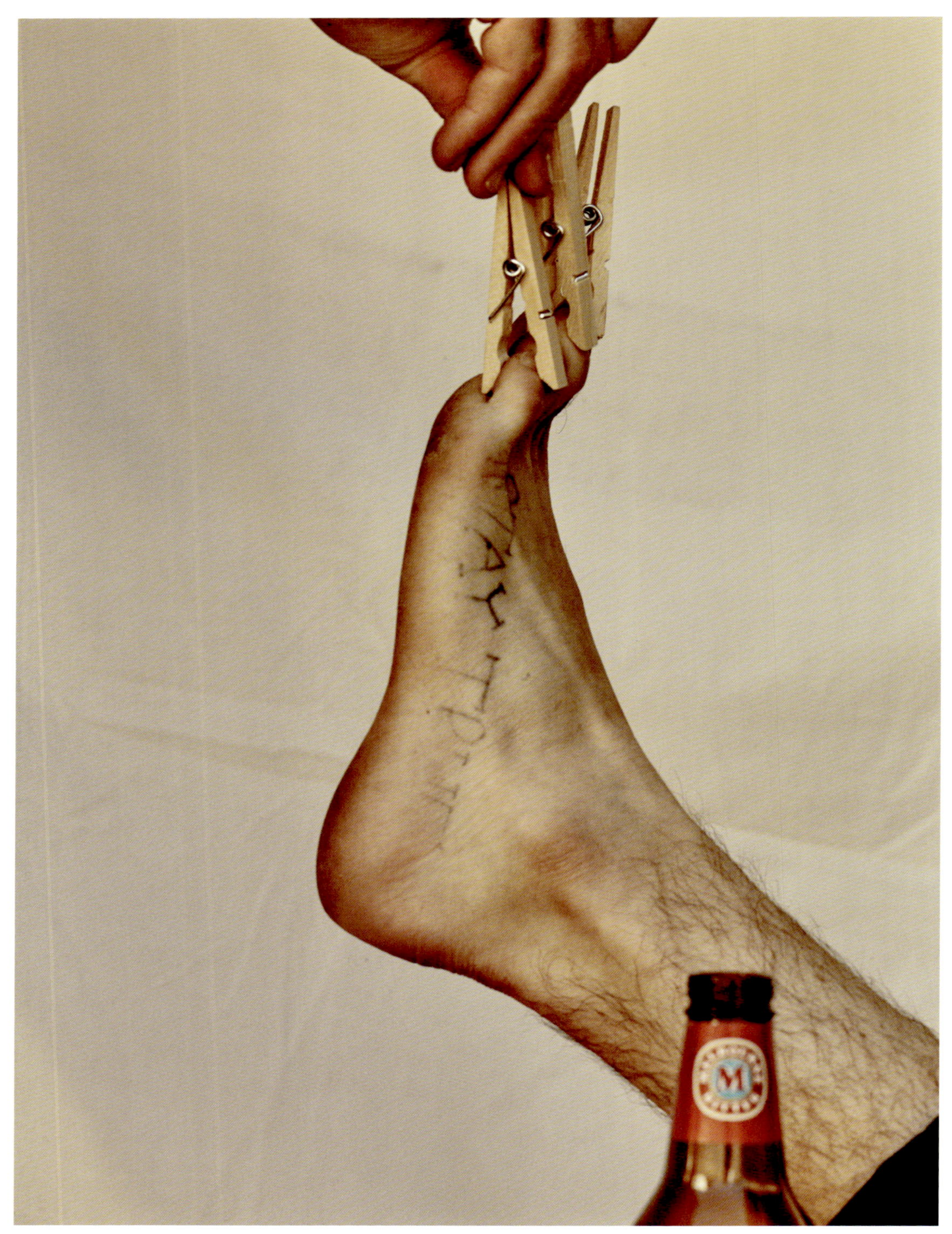

Peg and Toe. Moonee Ponds

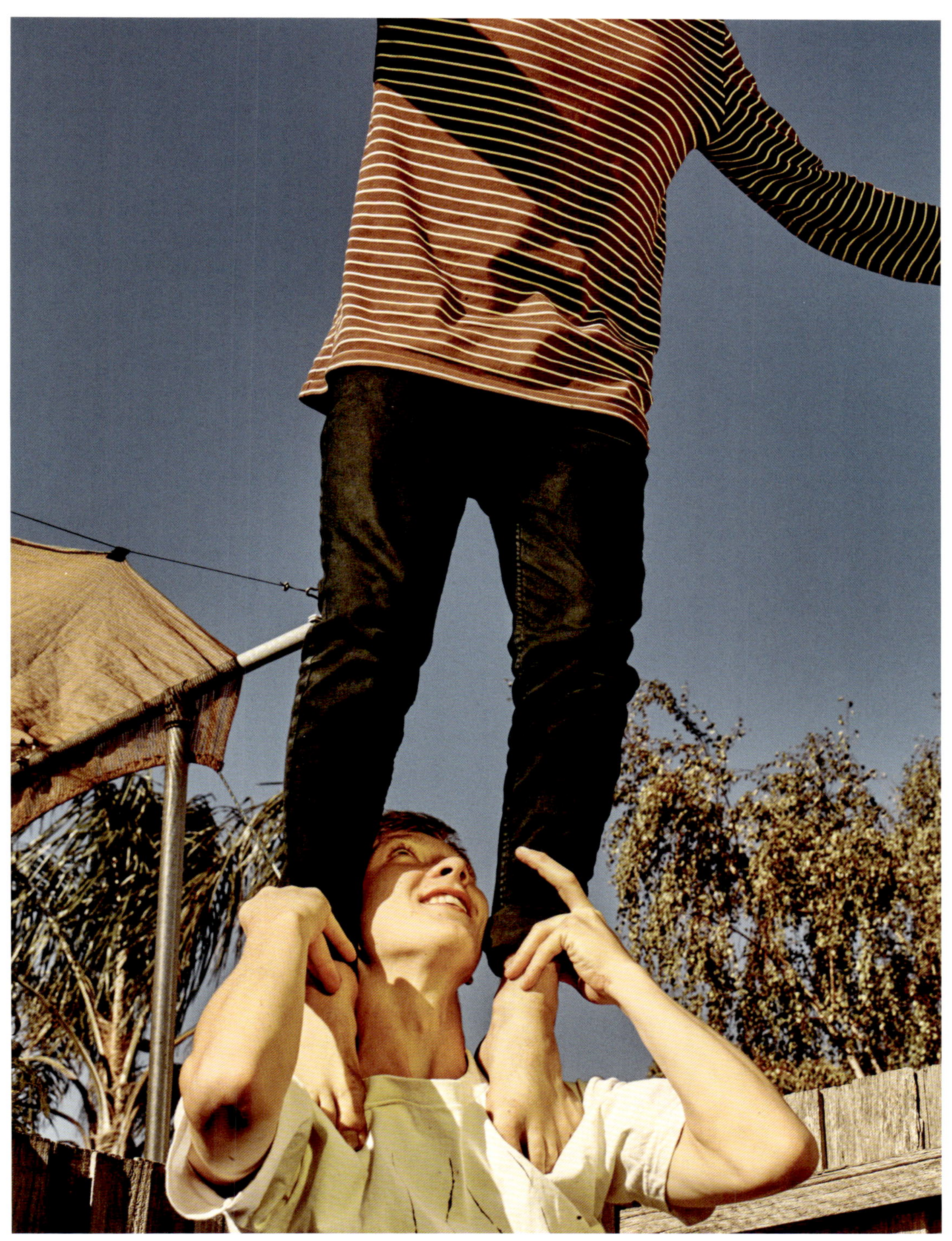

Kyle. Moonee Ponds

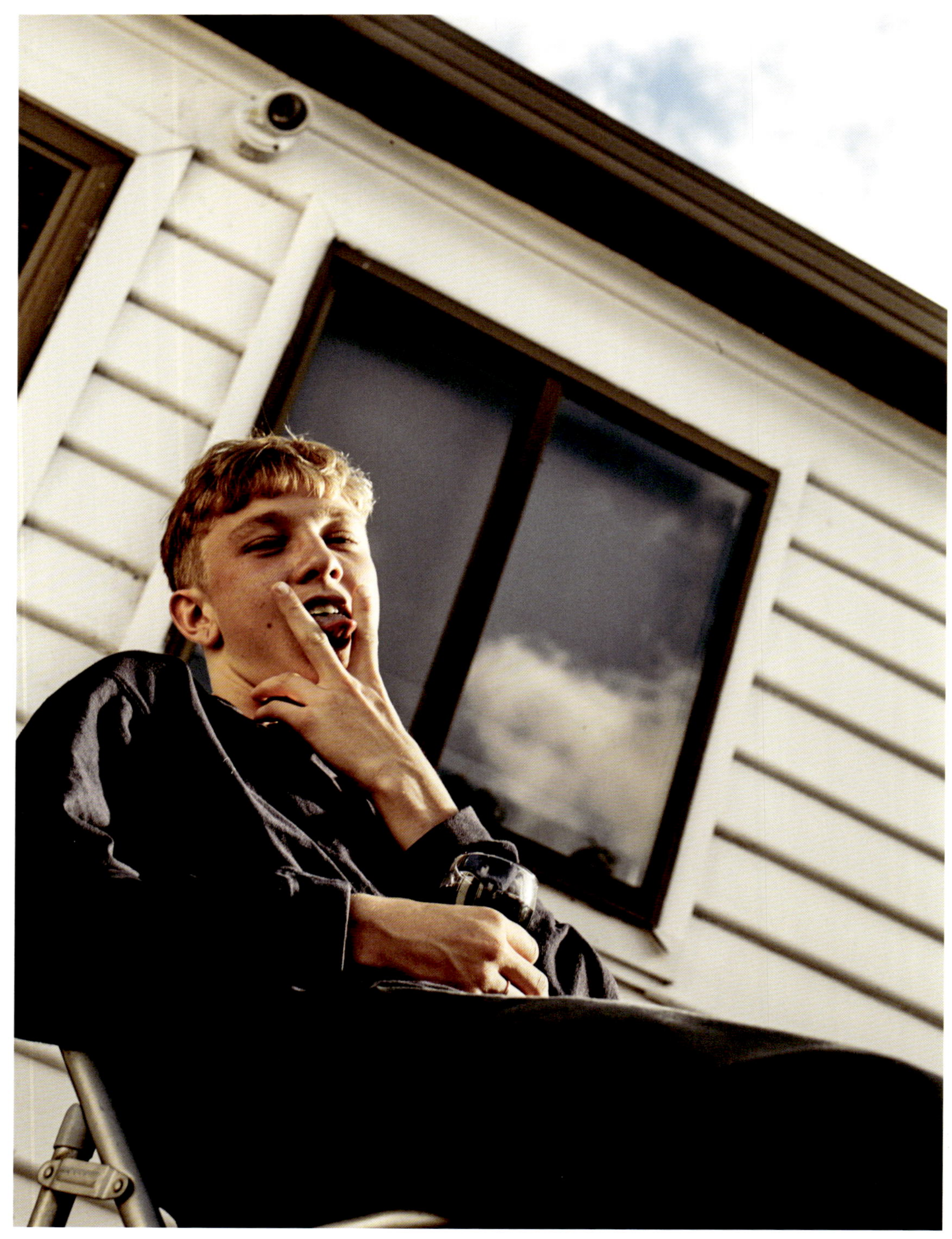

Kyle. Moonee Ponds

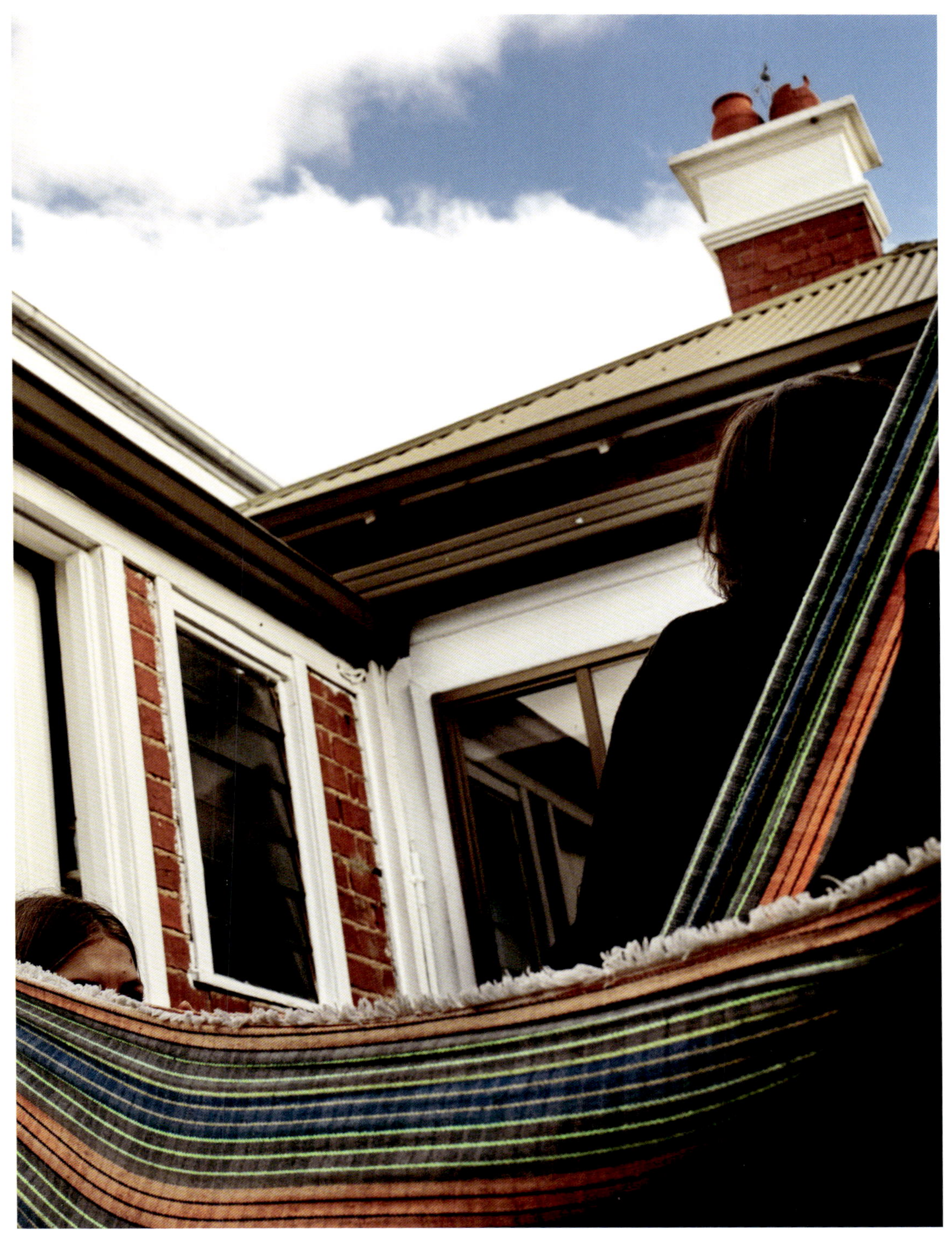

Hammock Party. Moonee Ponds

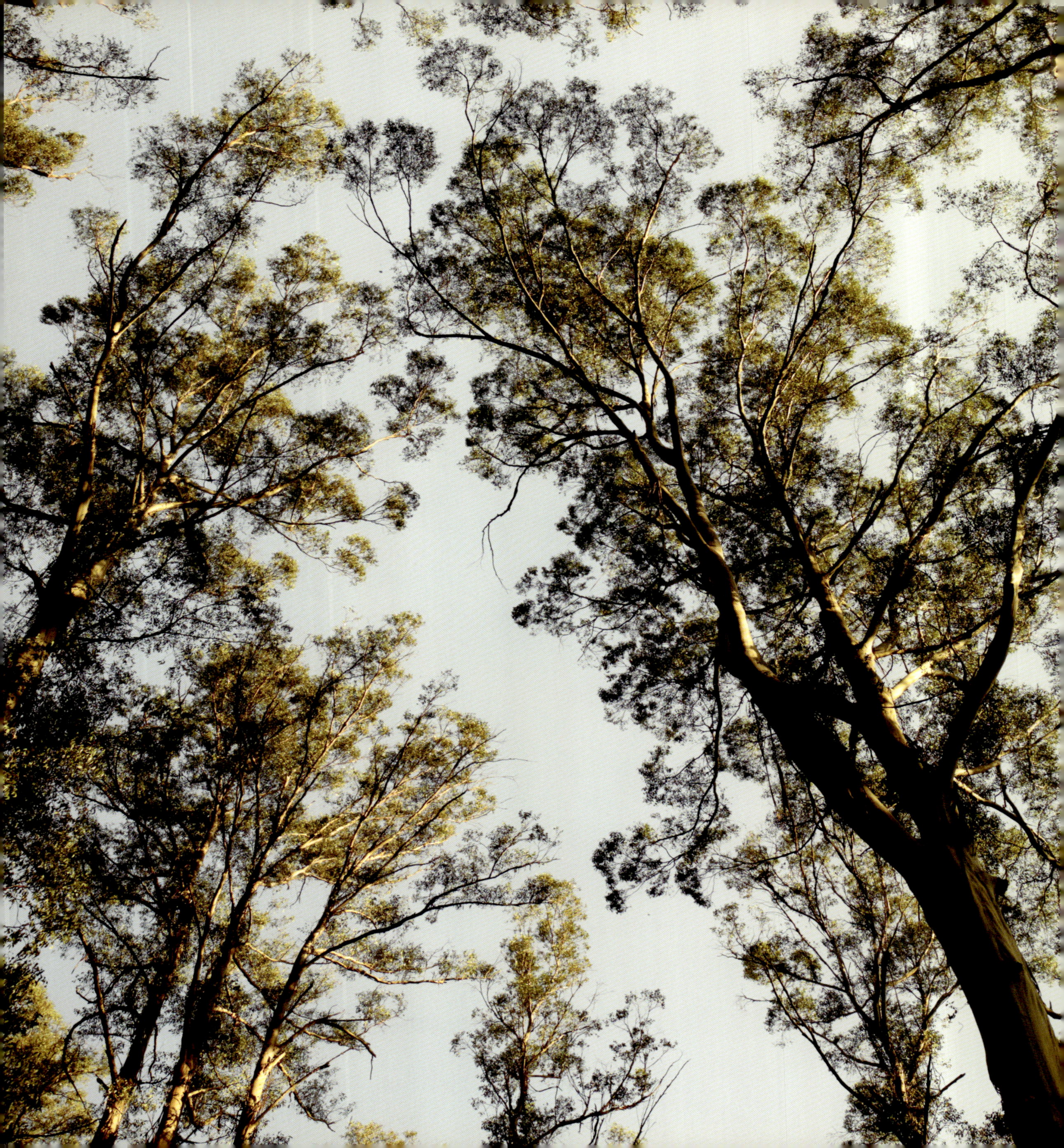

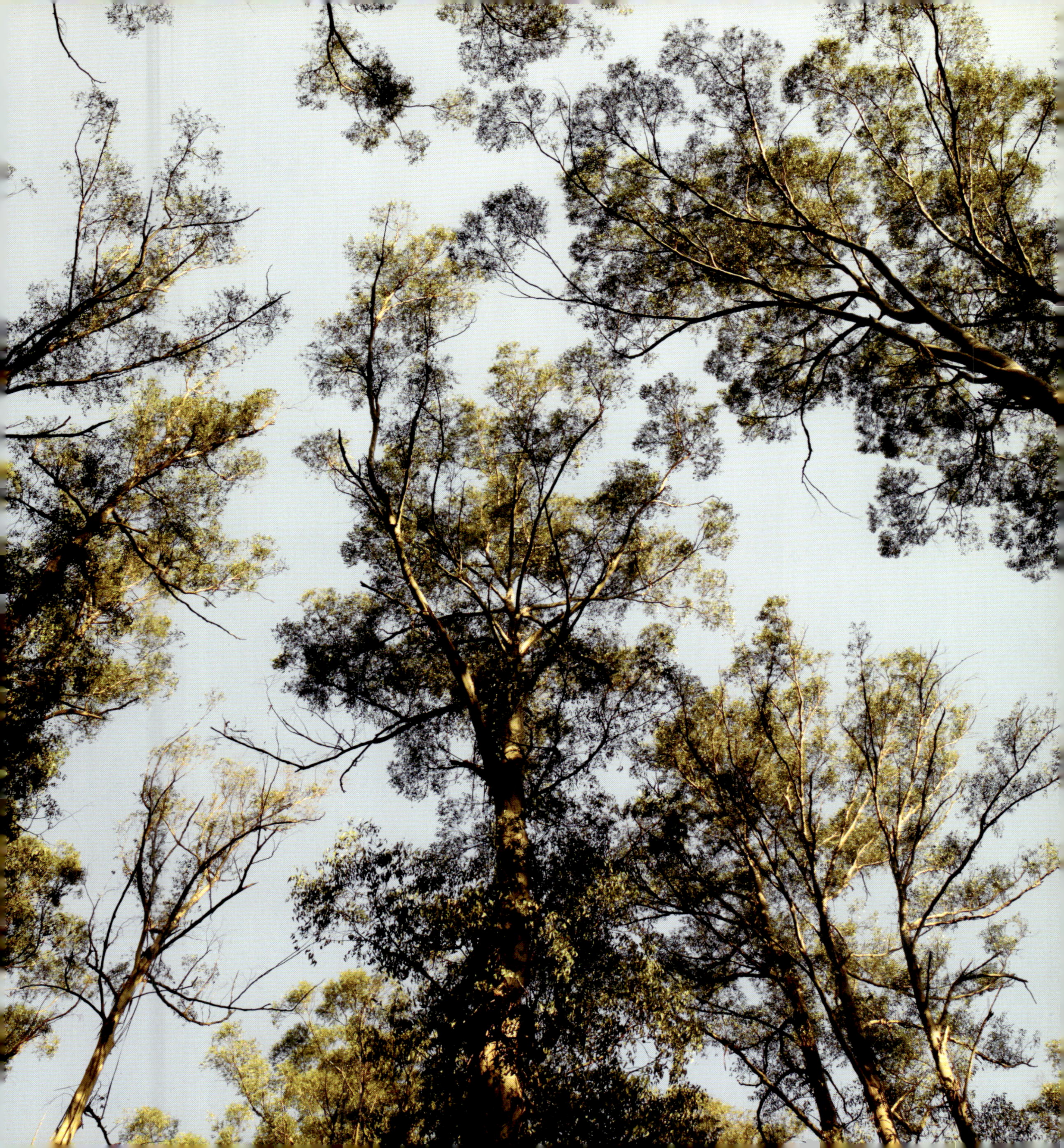

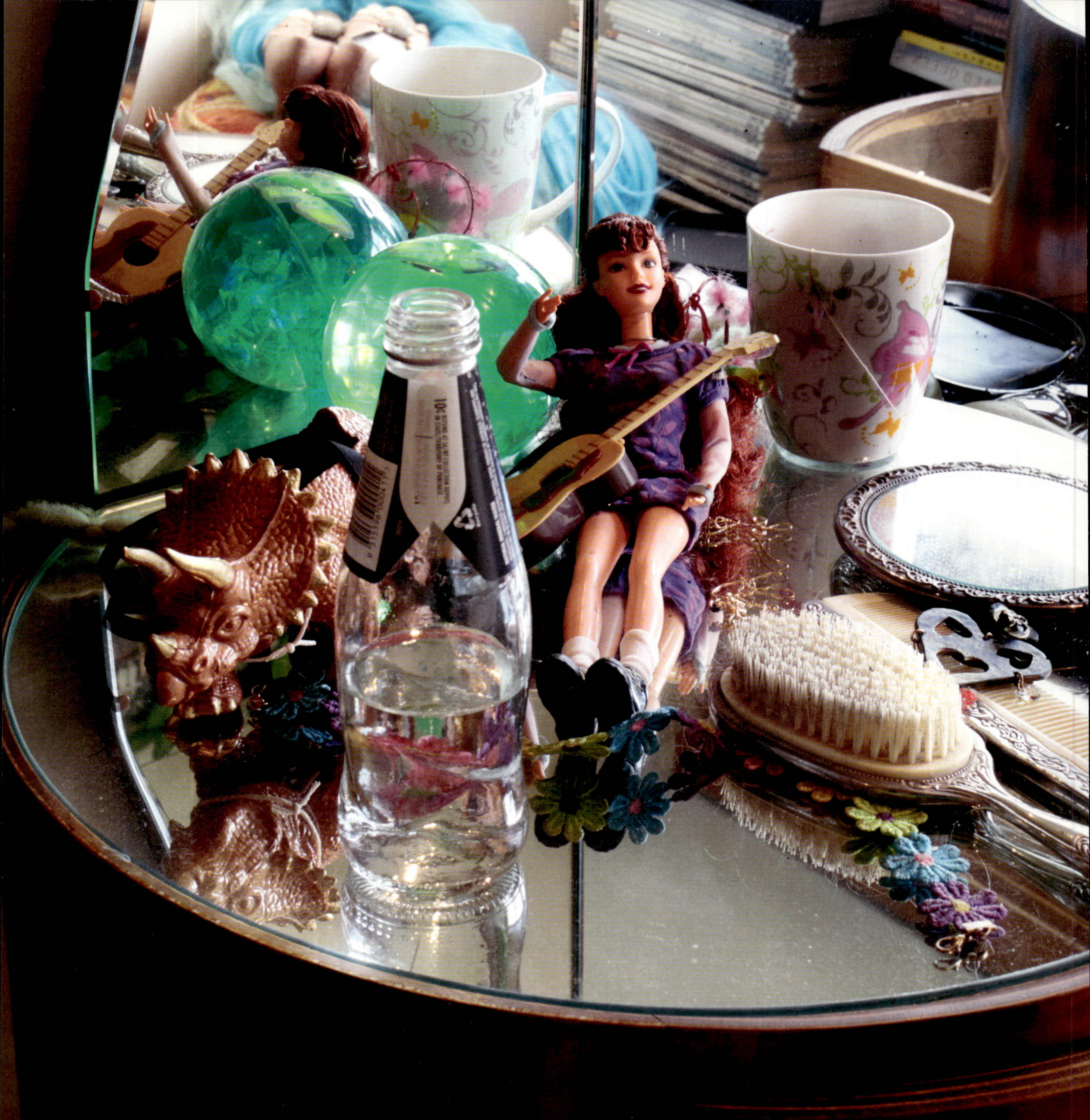

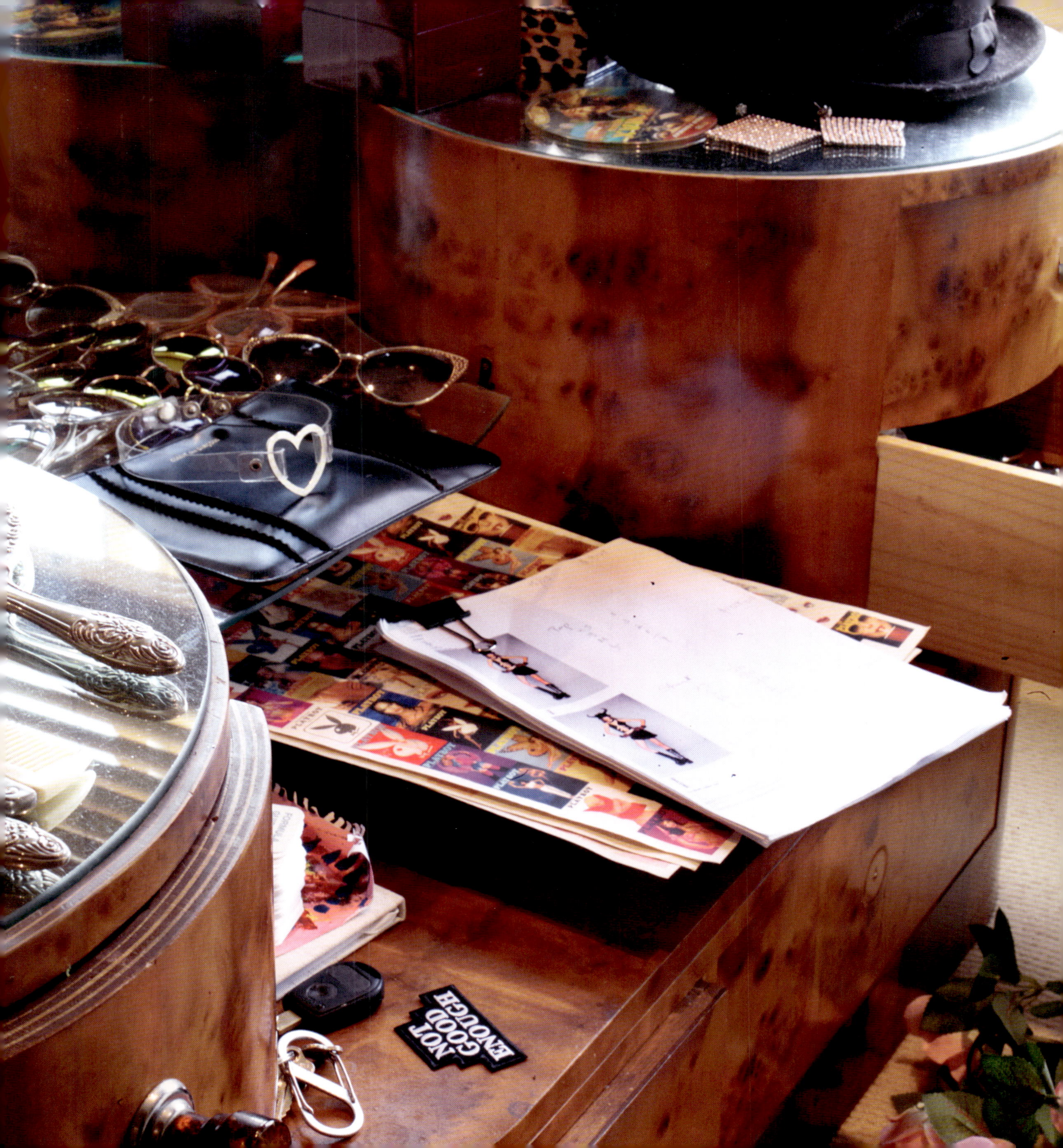

NOT GOOD ENOUGH

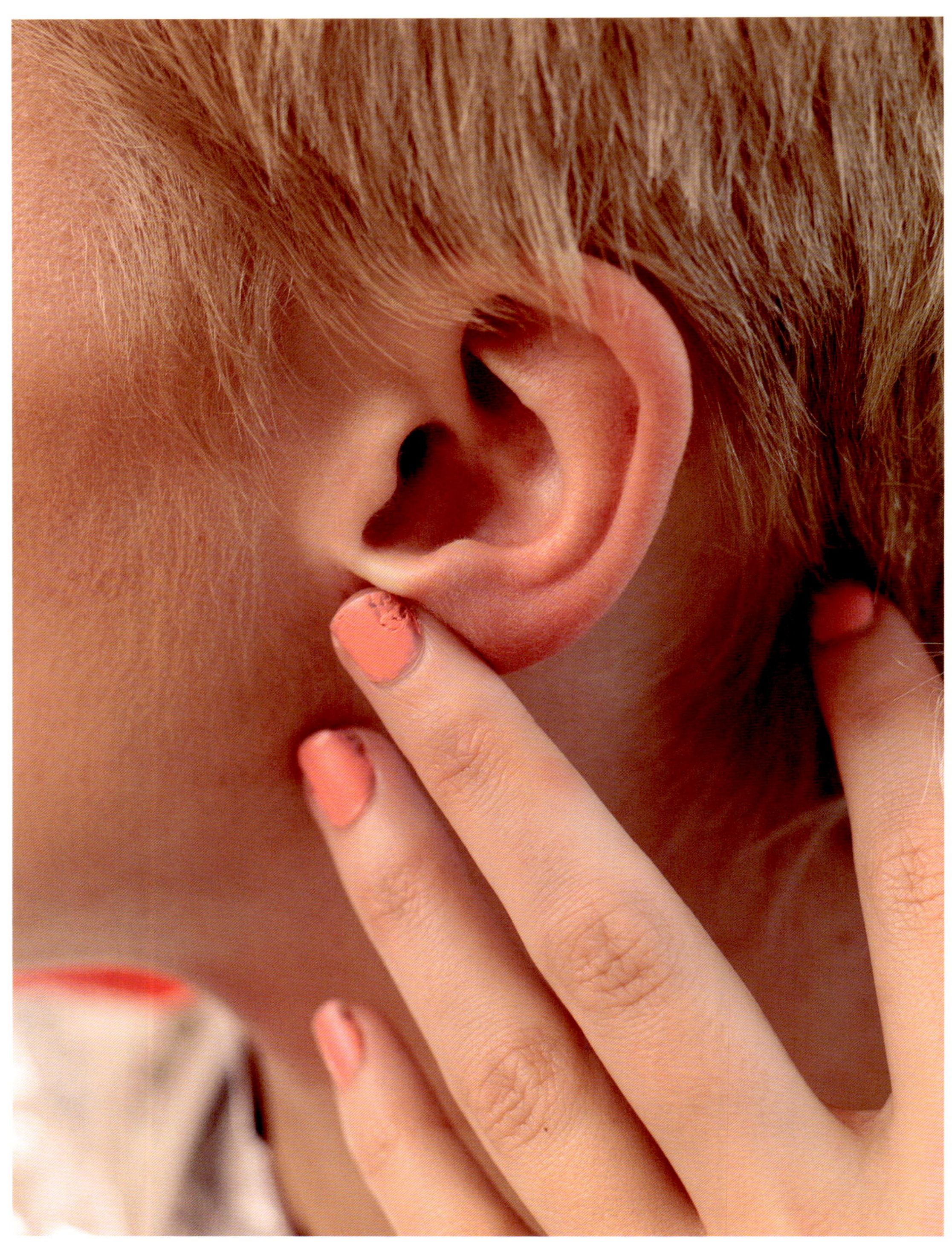

Nail paint. Home of Moosedoll

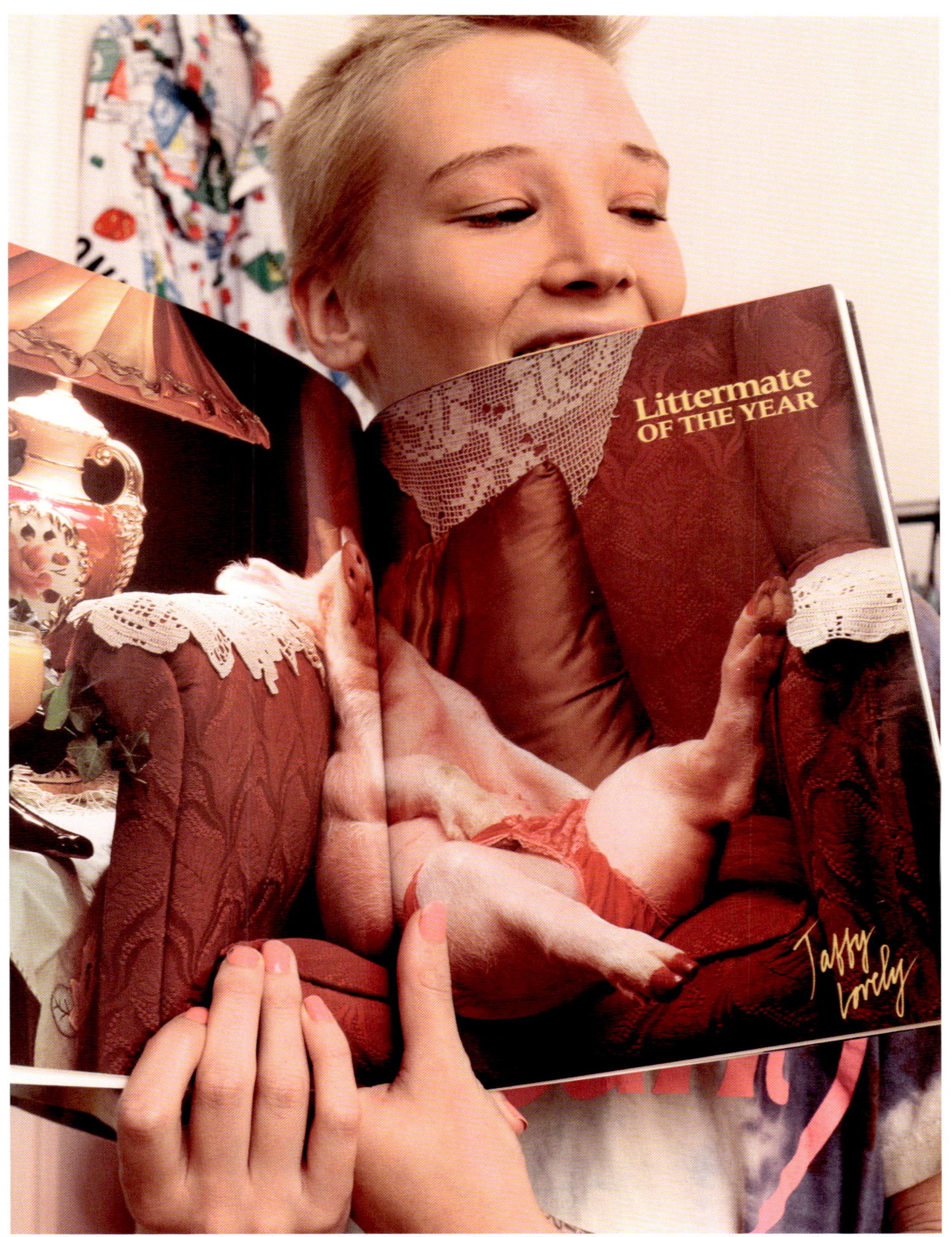

Pig Porn. Home of Moosedoll

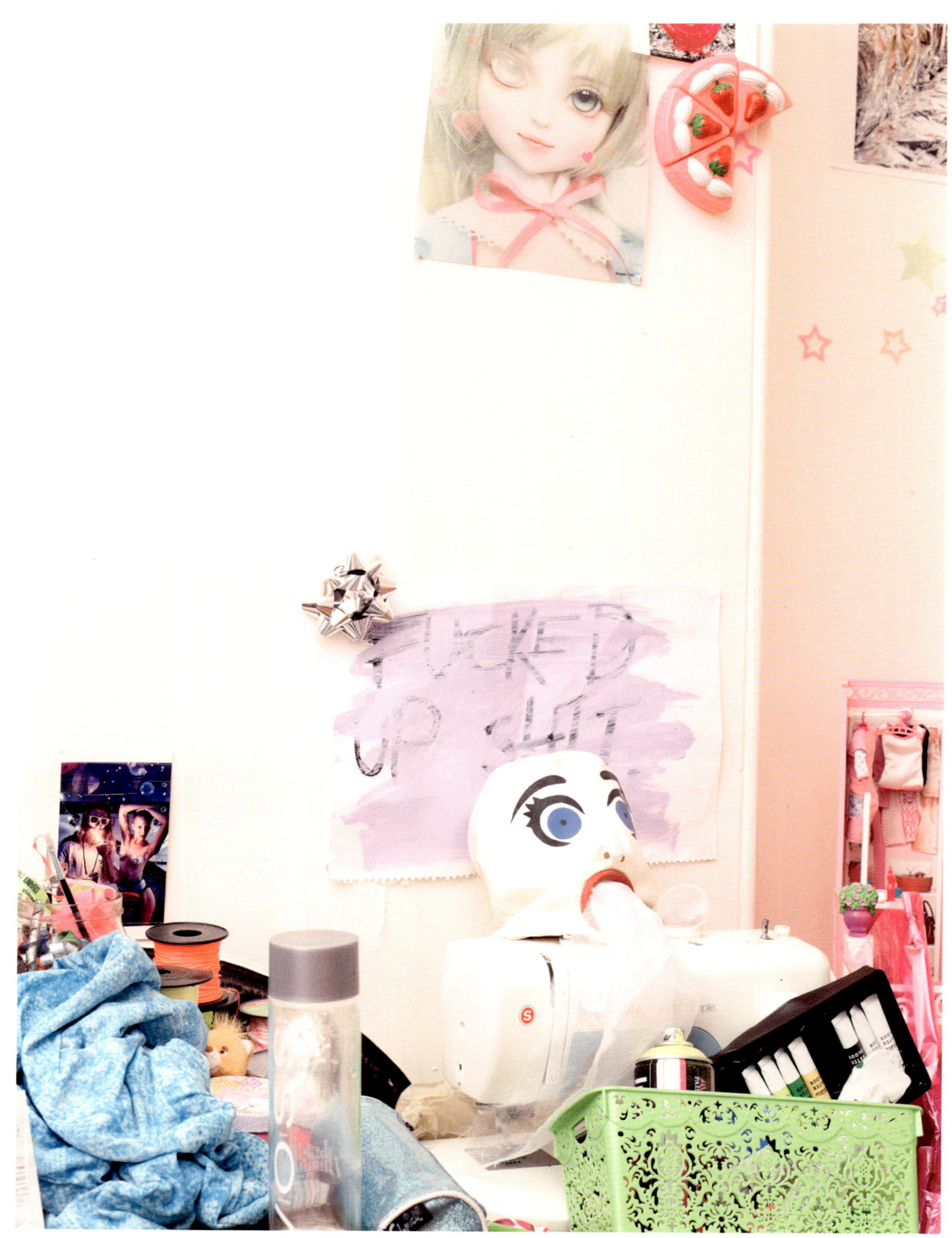

Camera left. Home of Moosedoll

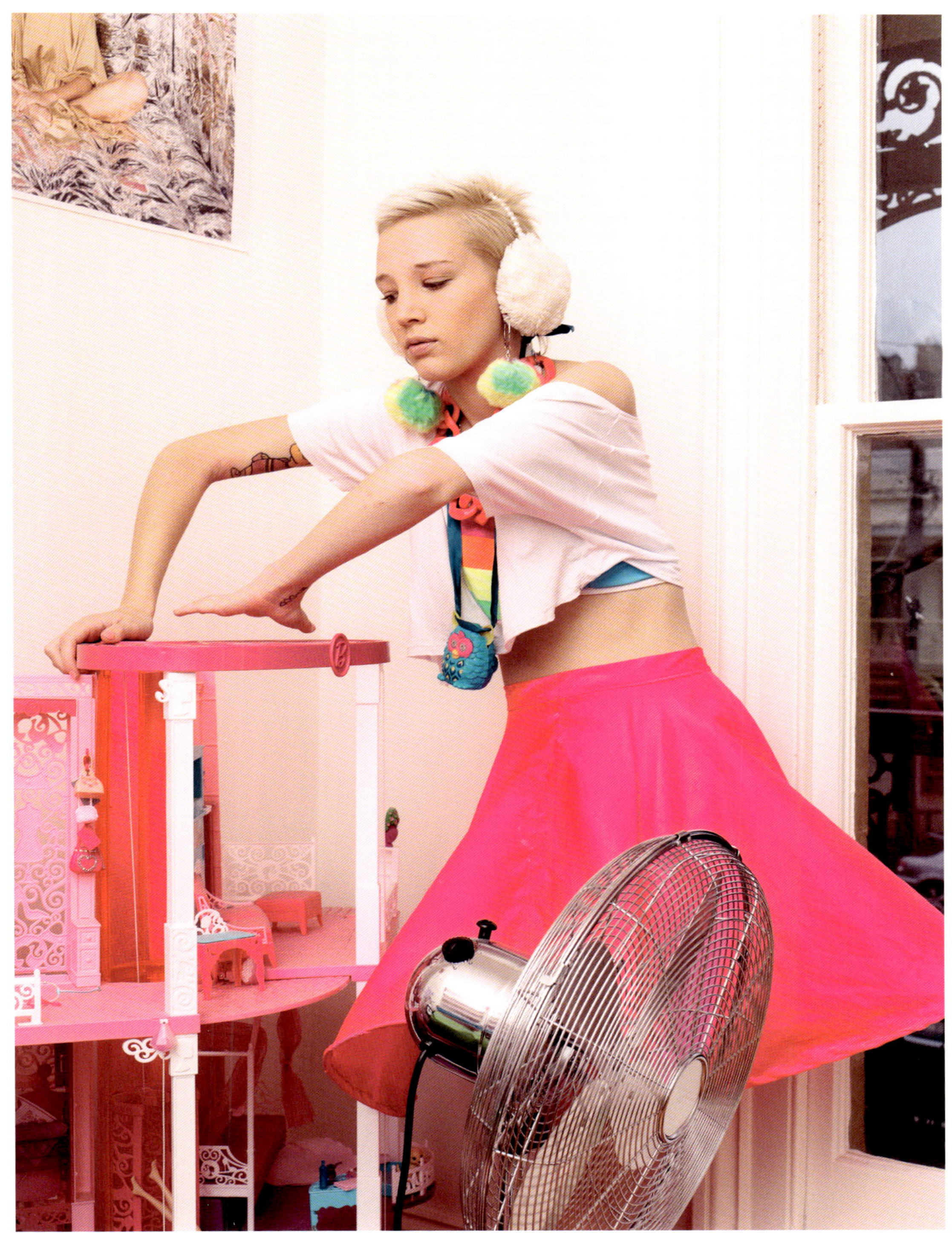

Camera right. Home of Moosedoll

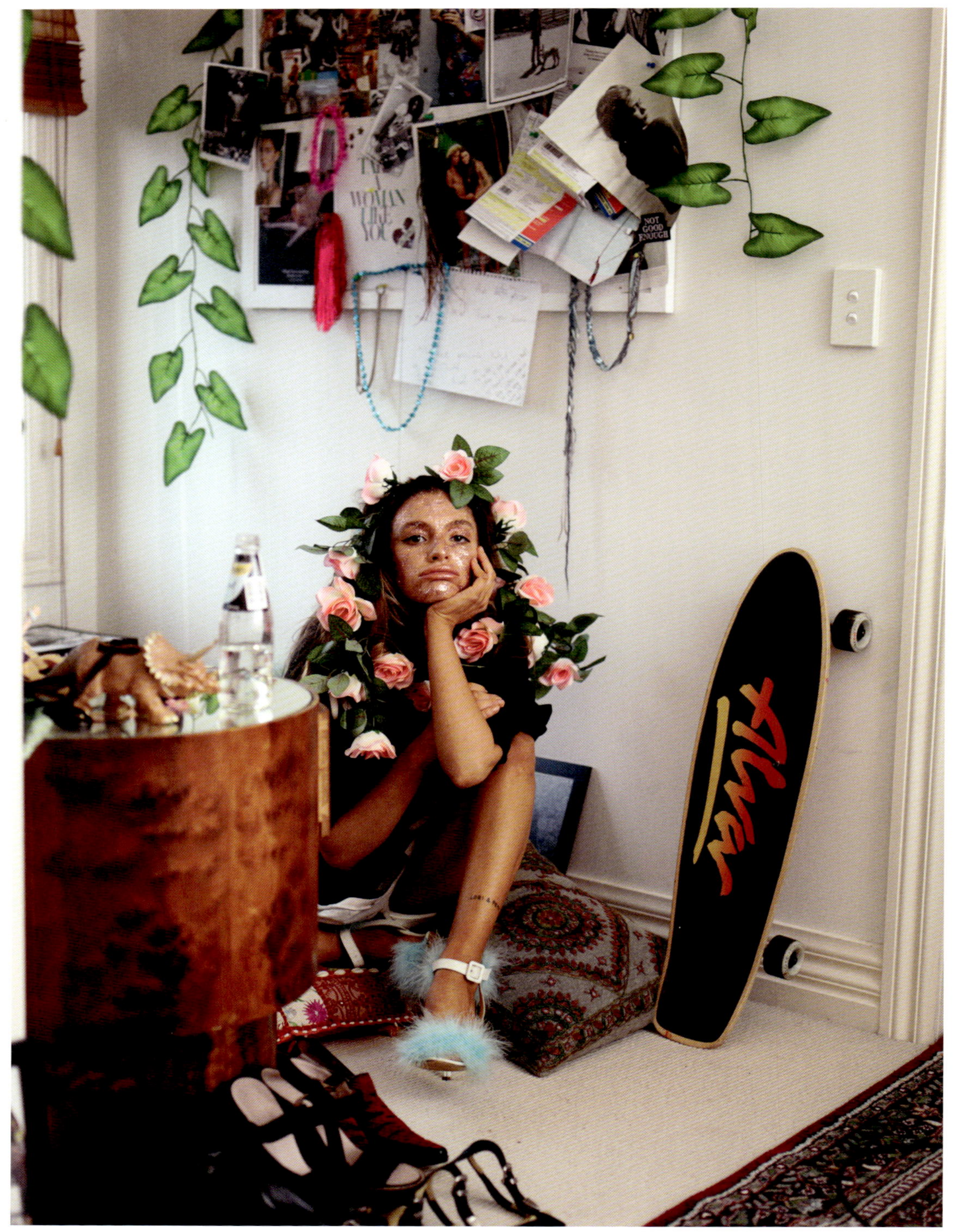

Suga Possum. Balwyn

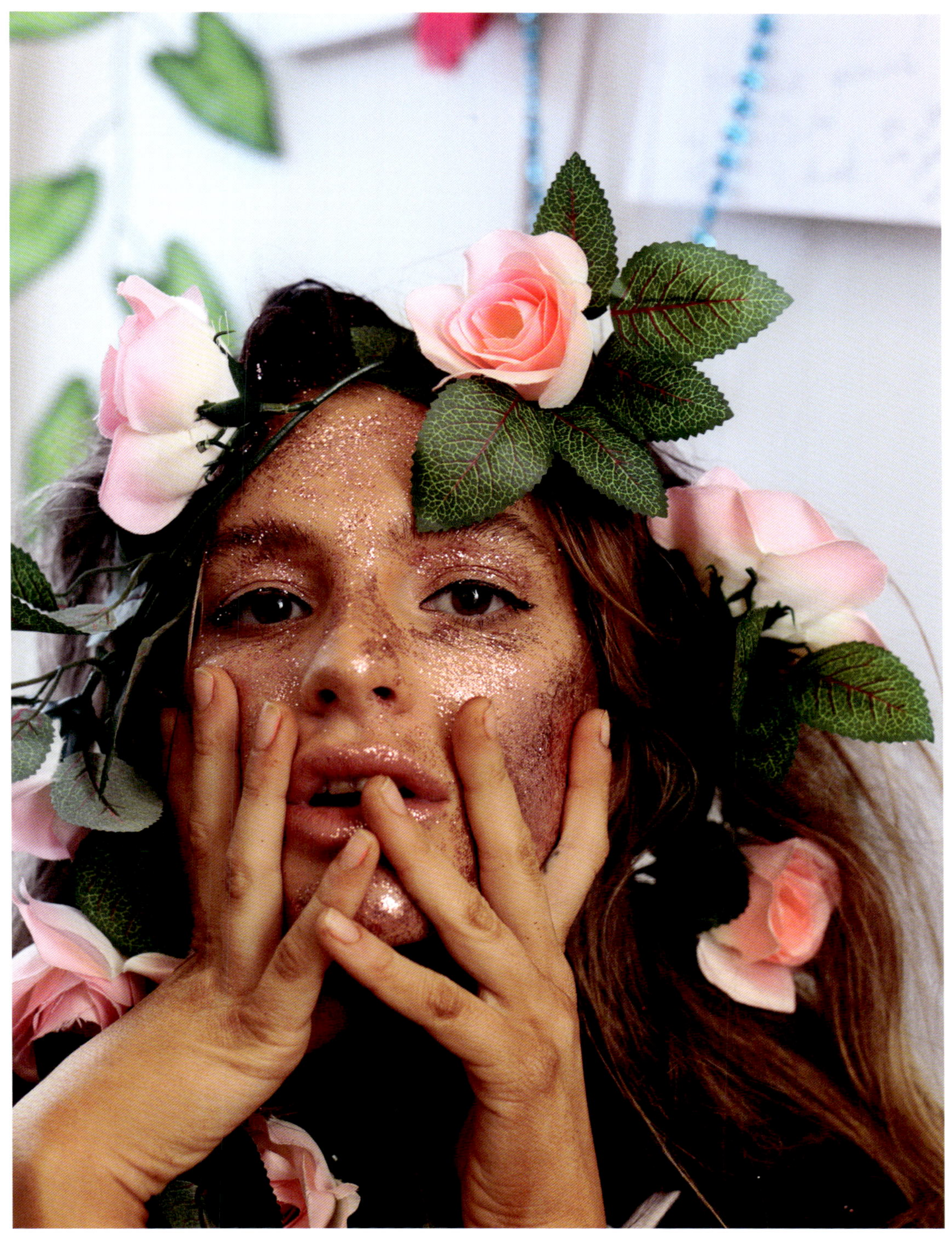

Suga Possum. Balwyn

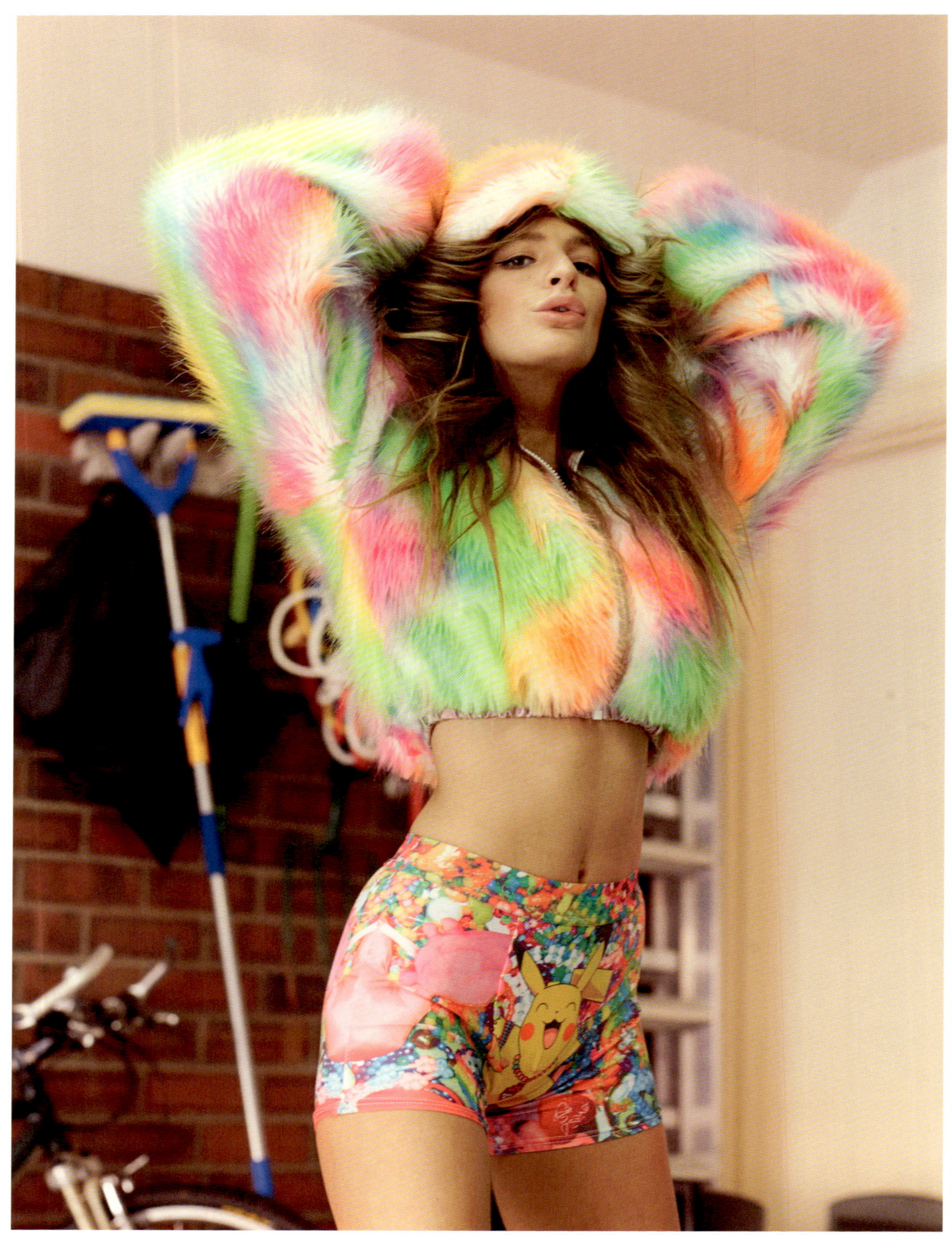

Suga Possum. Balwyn

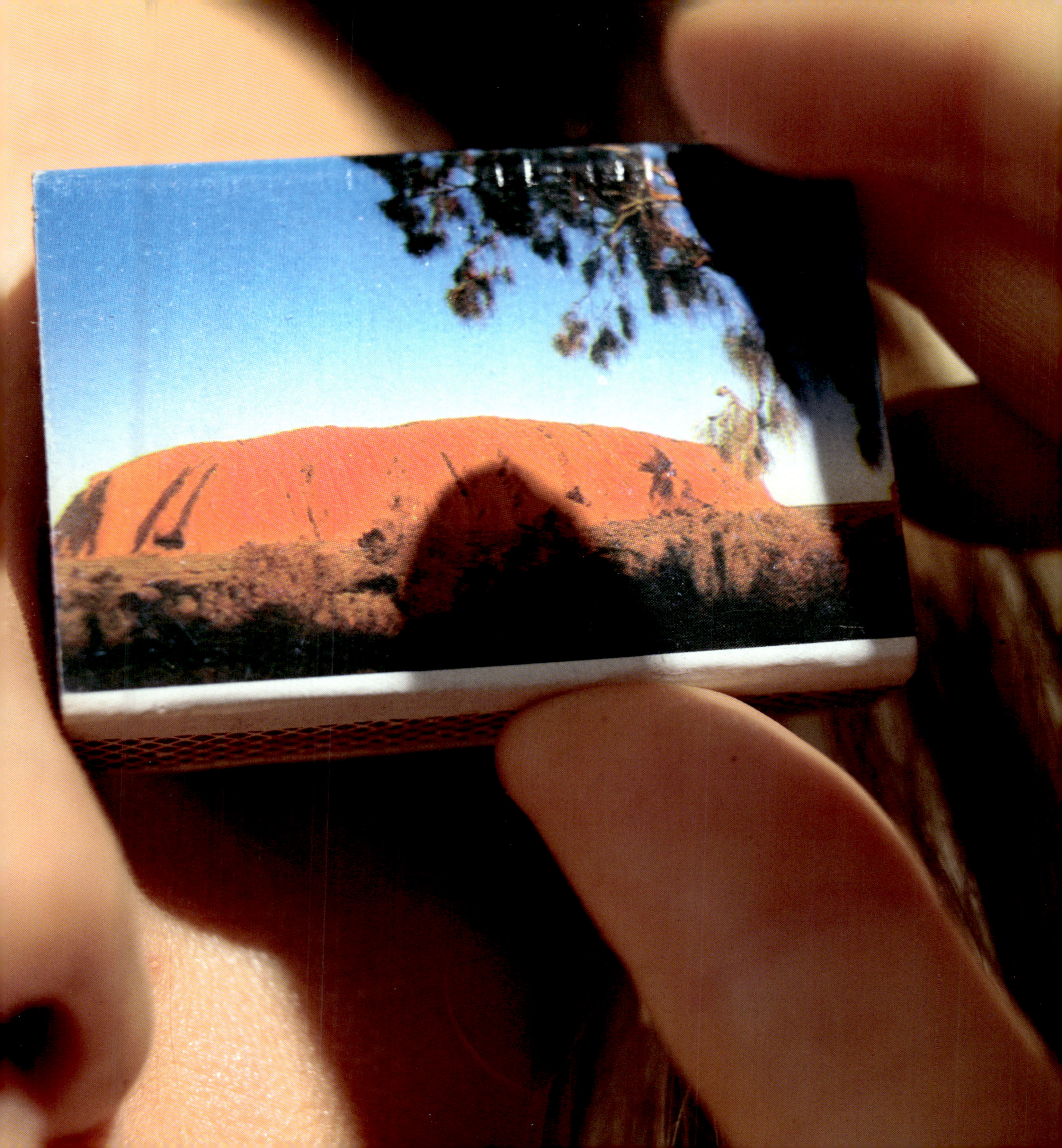

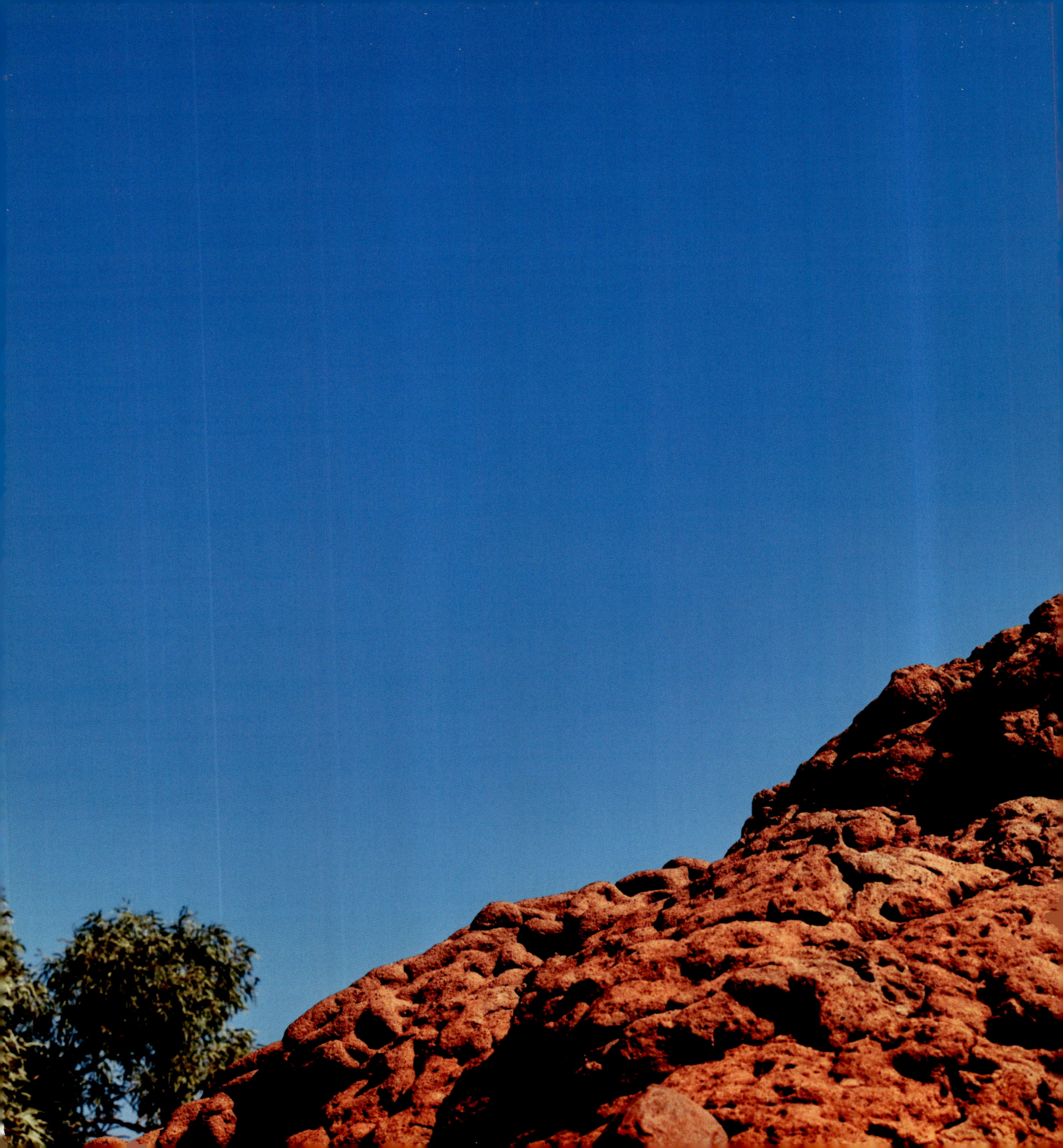

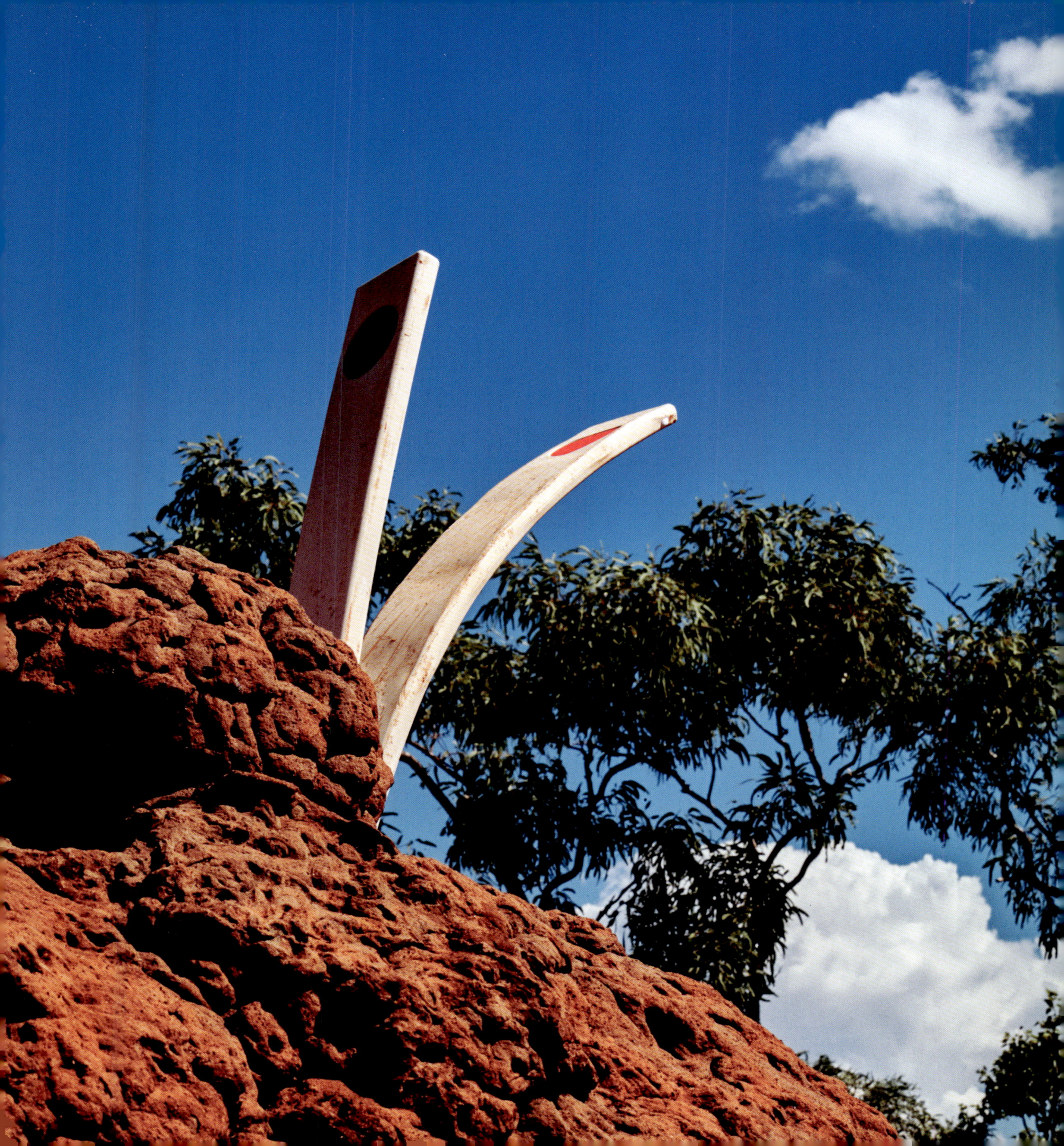

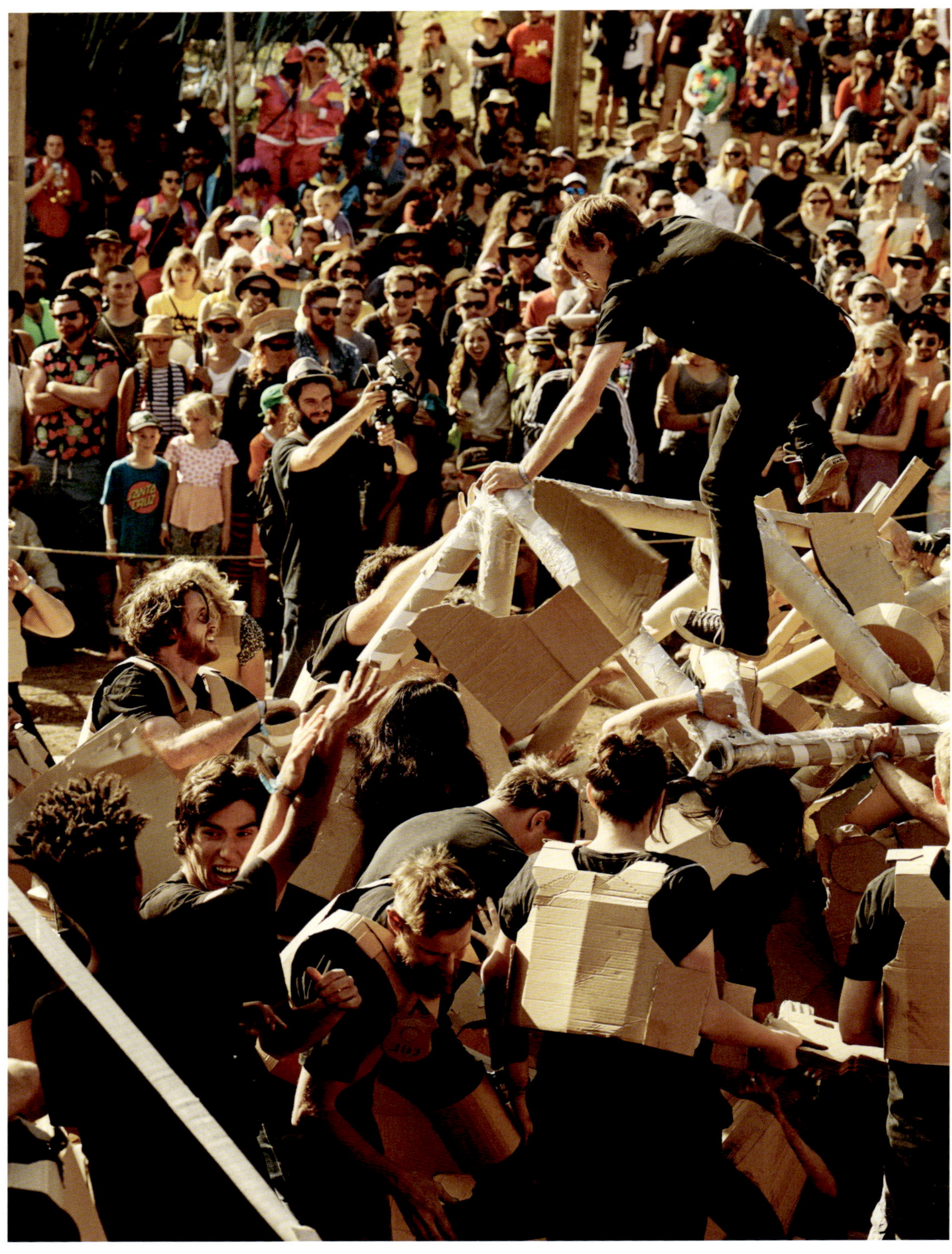

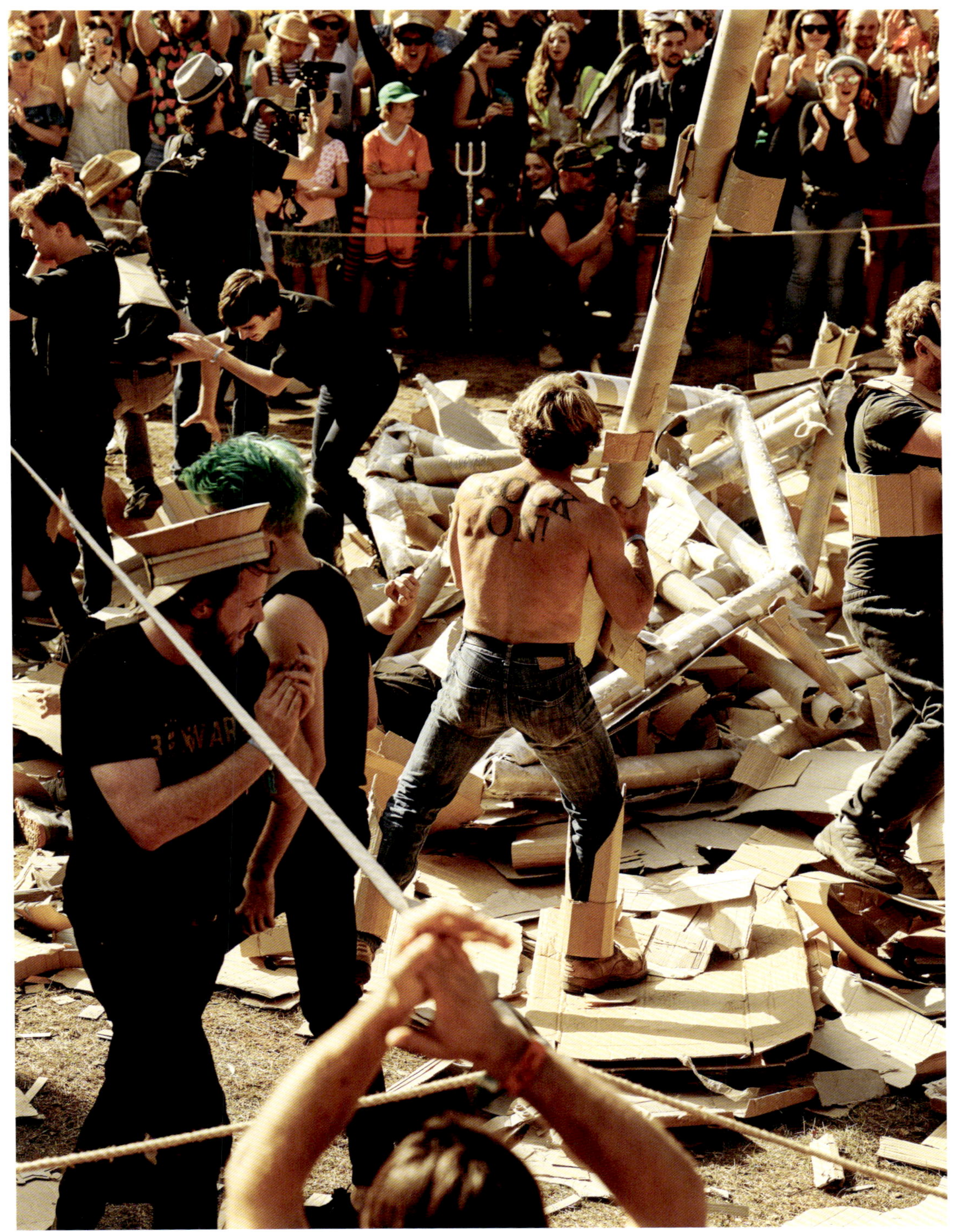

BoxWars. Boogie

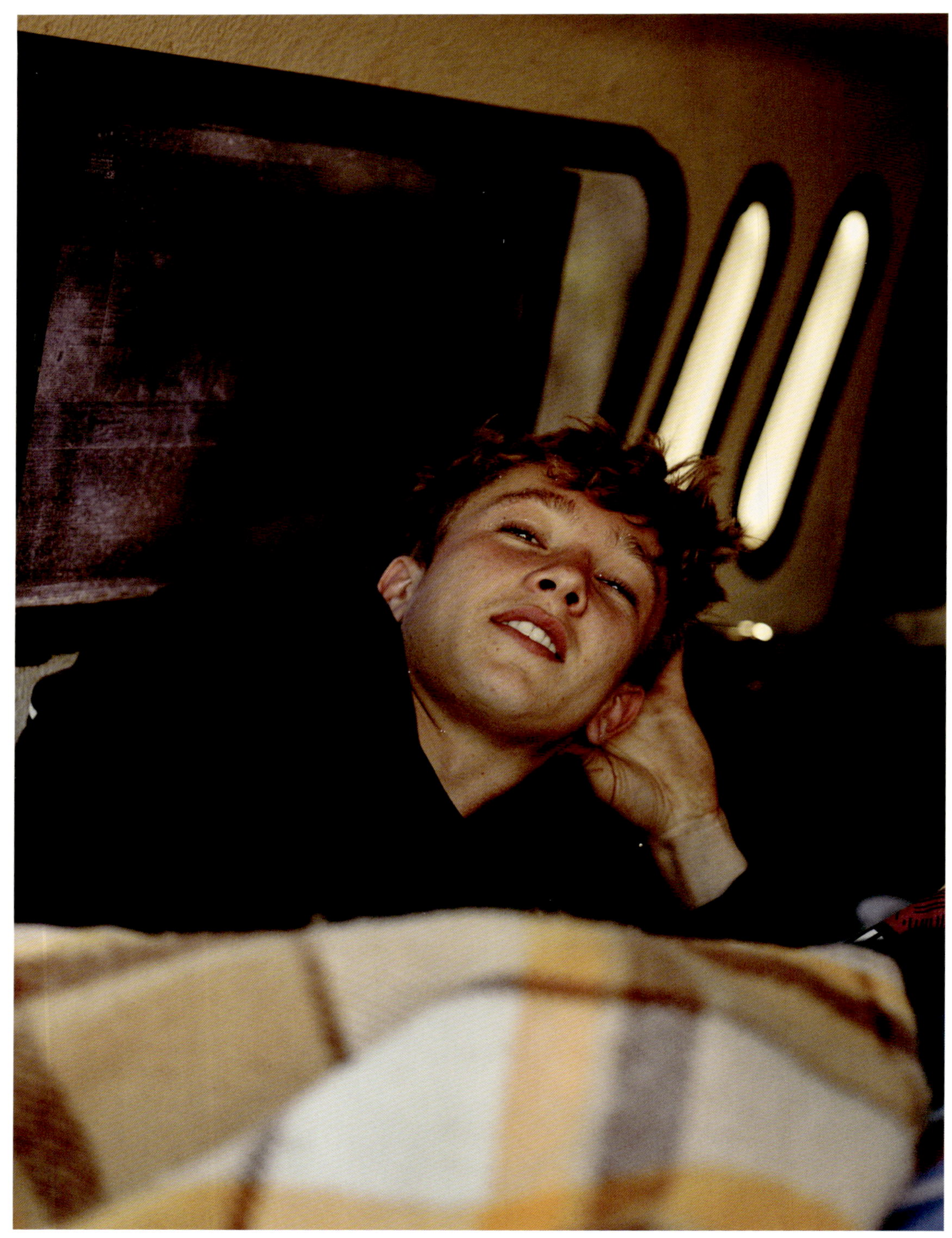

Kyle. Boogie

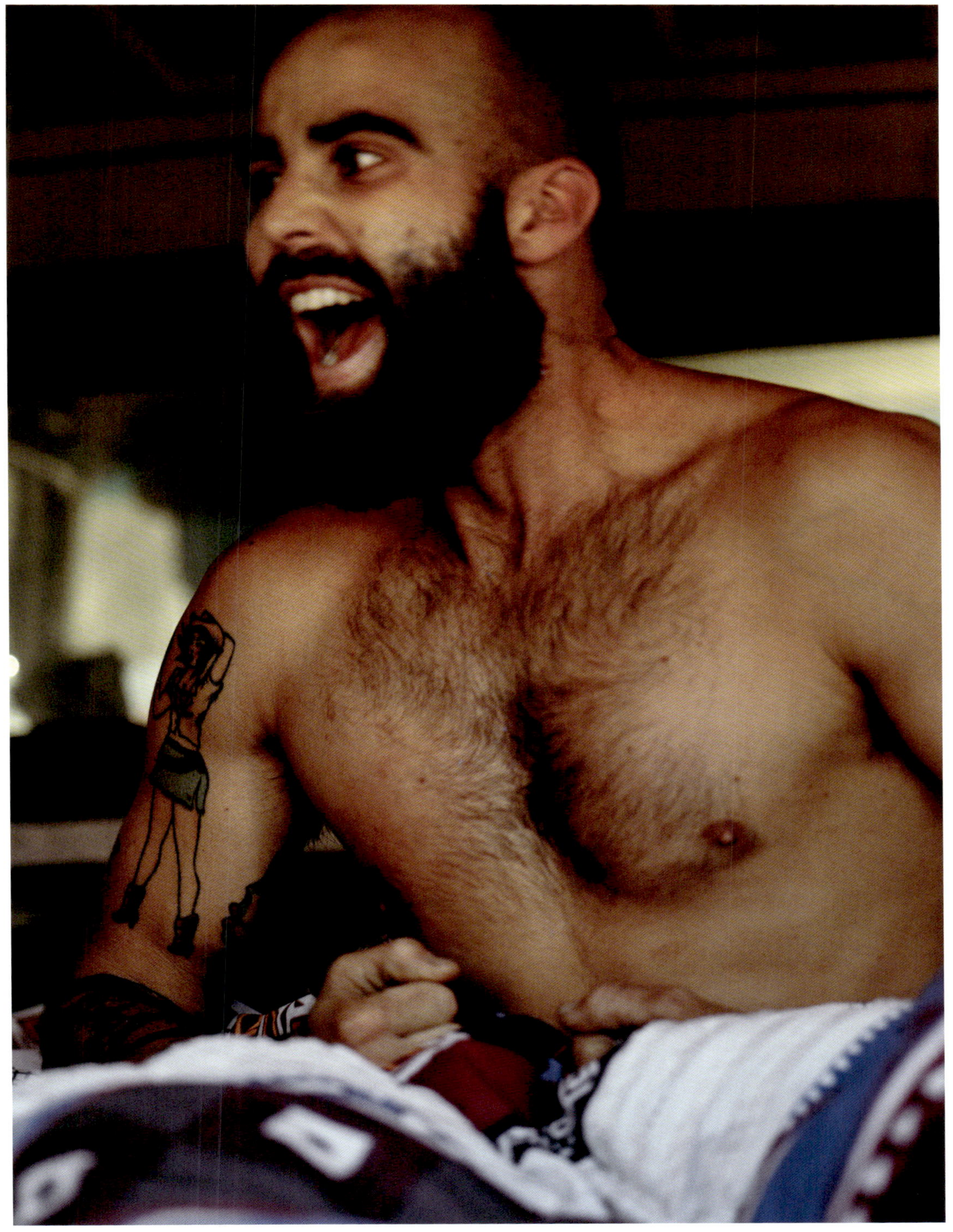

Juicy. Boogie

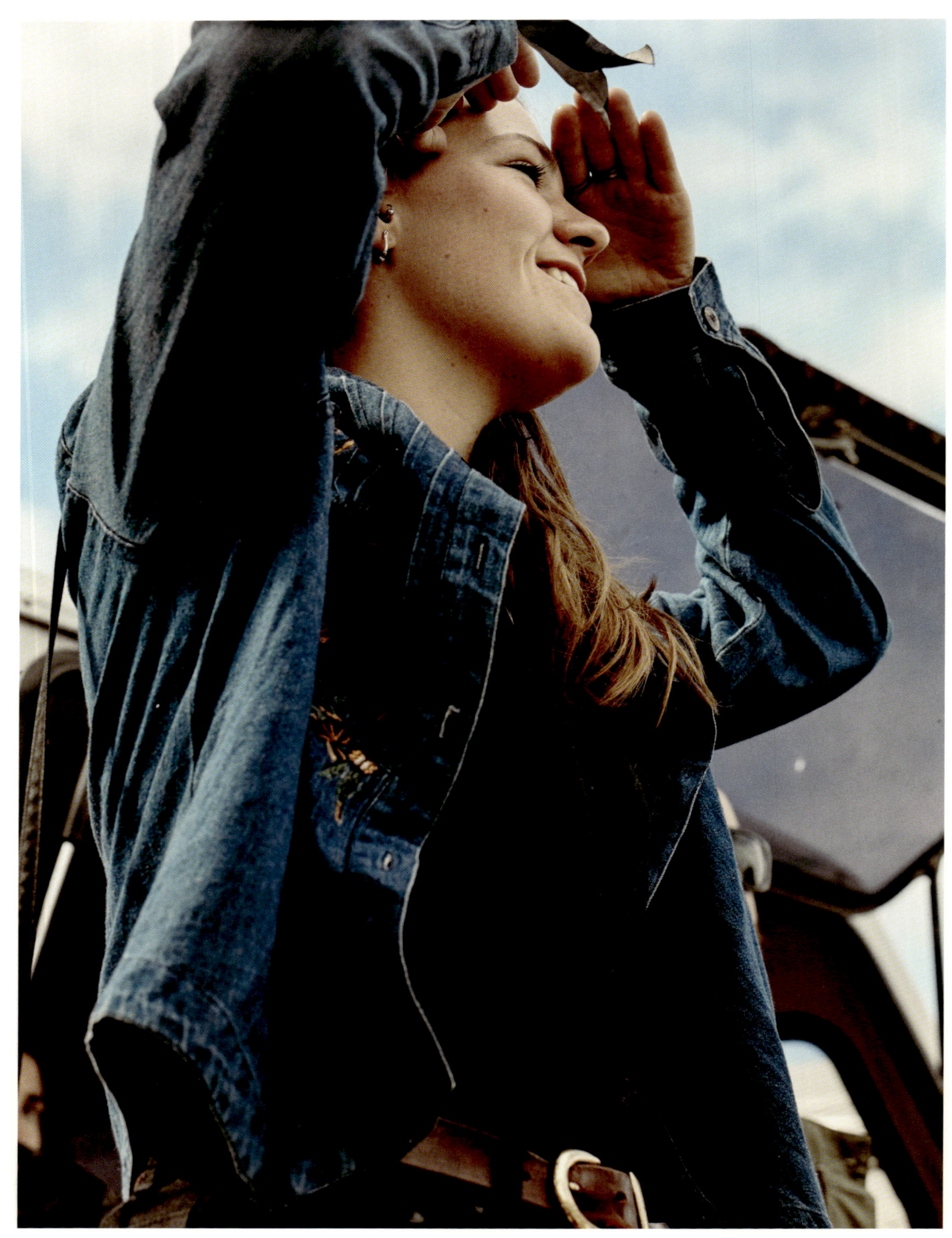

Lookout. Boogie

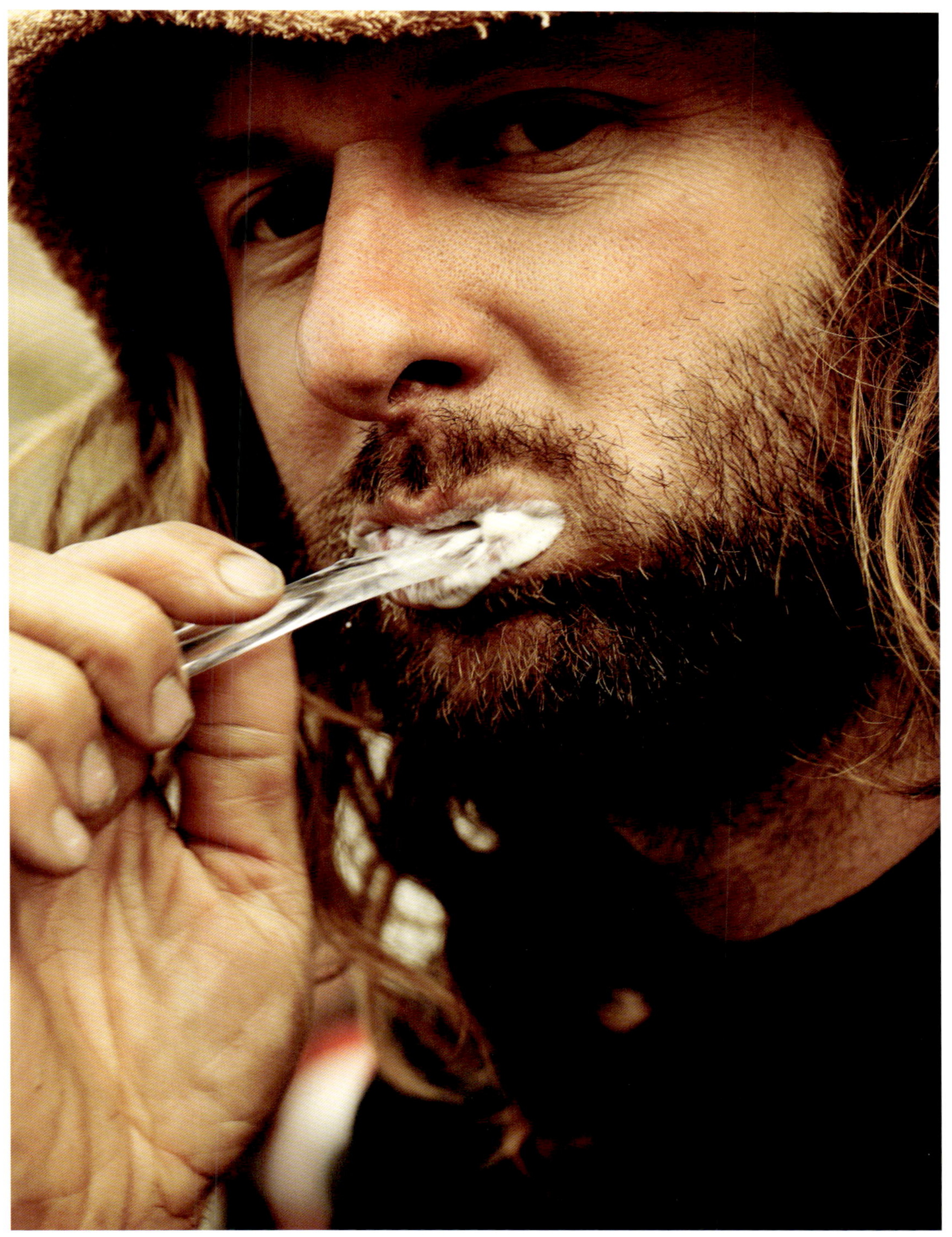

T-Bone. Boogie

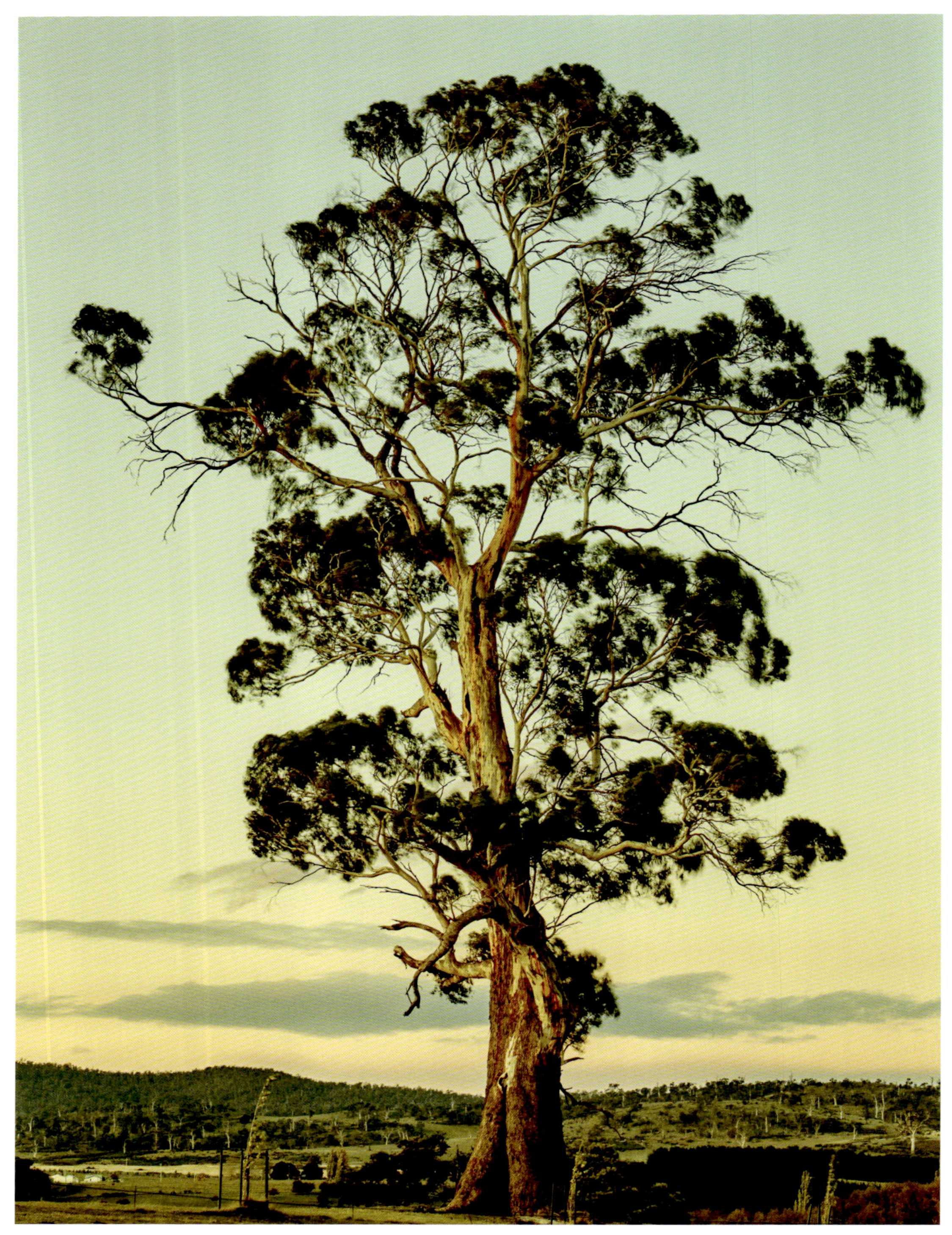

Carrick. Tasmania

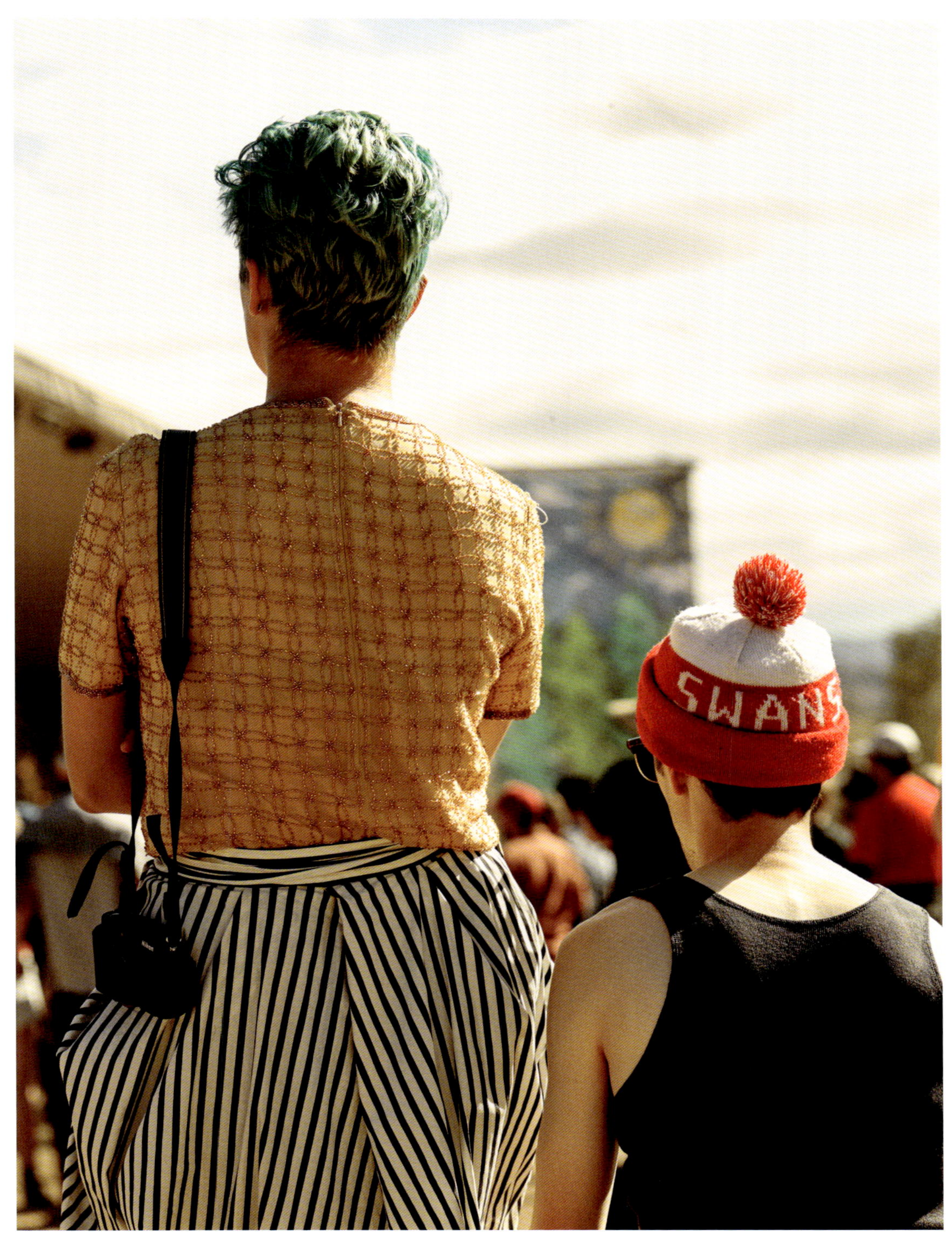

Main stage. Boogie

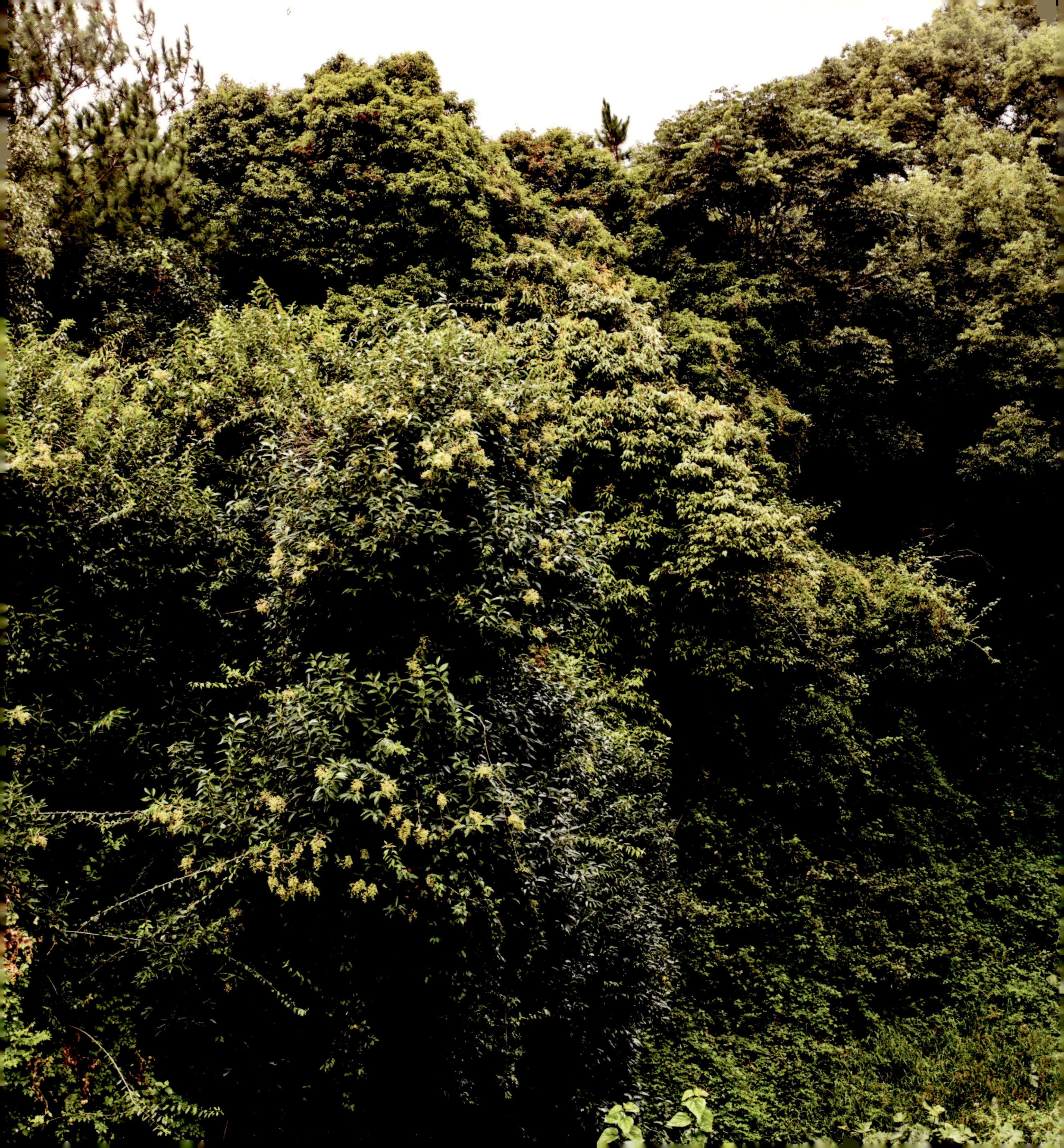

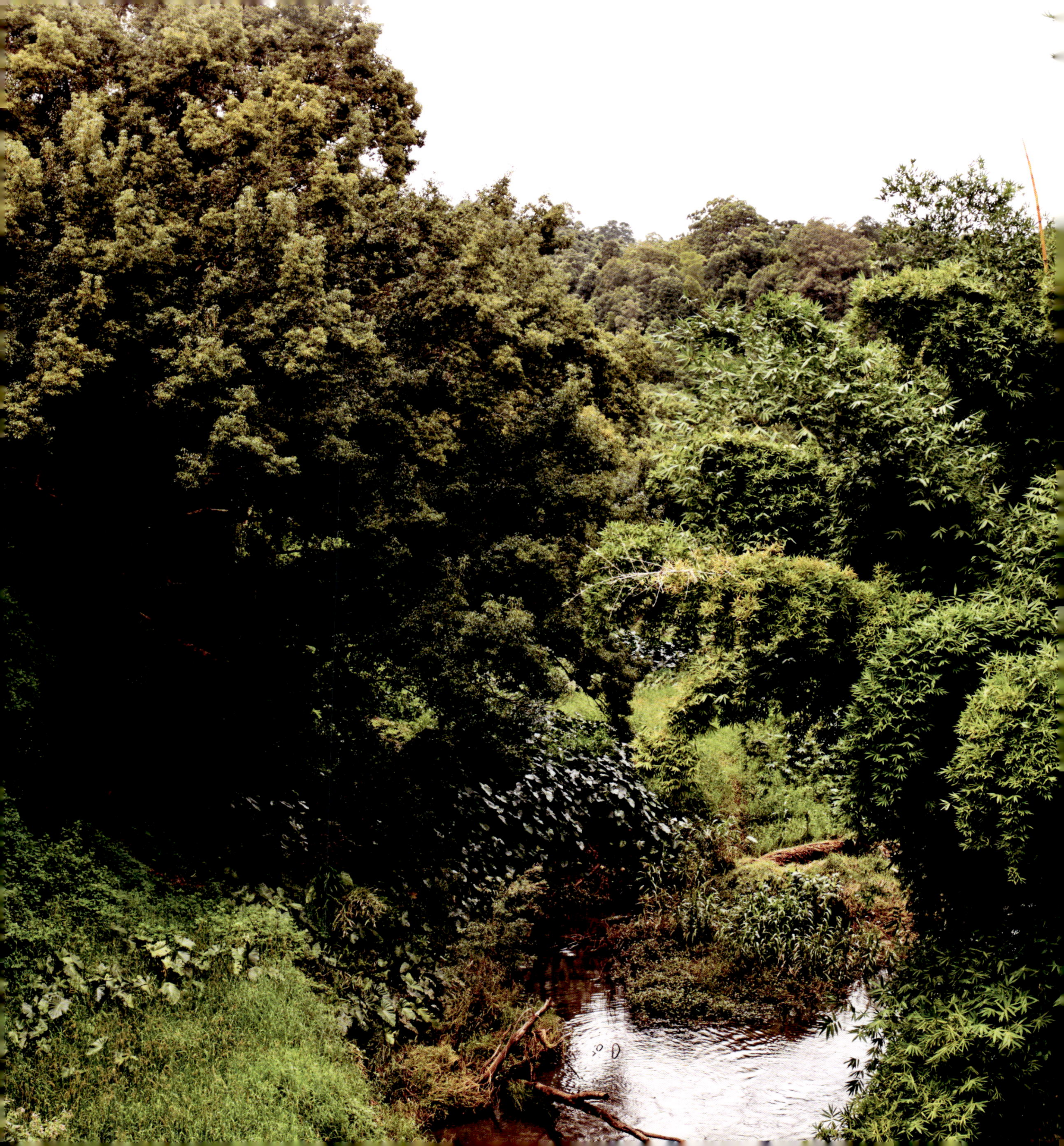

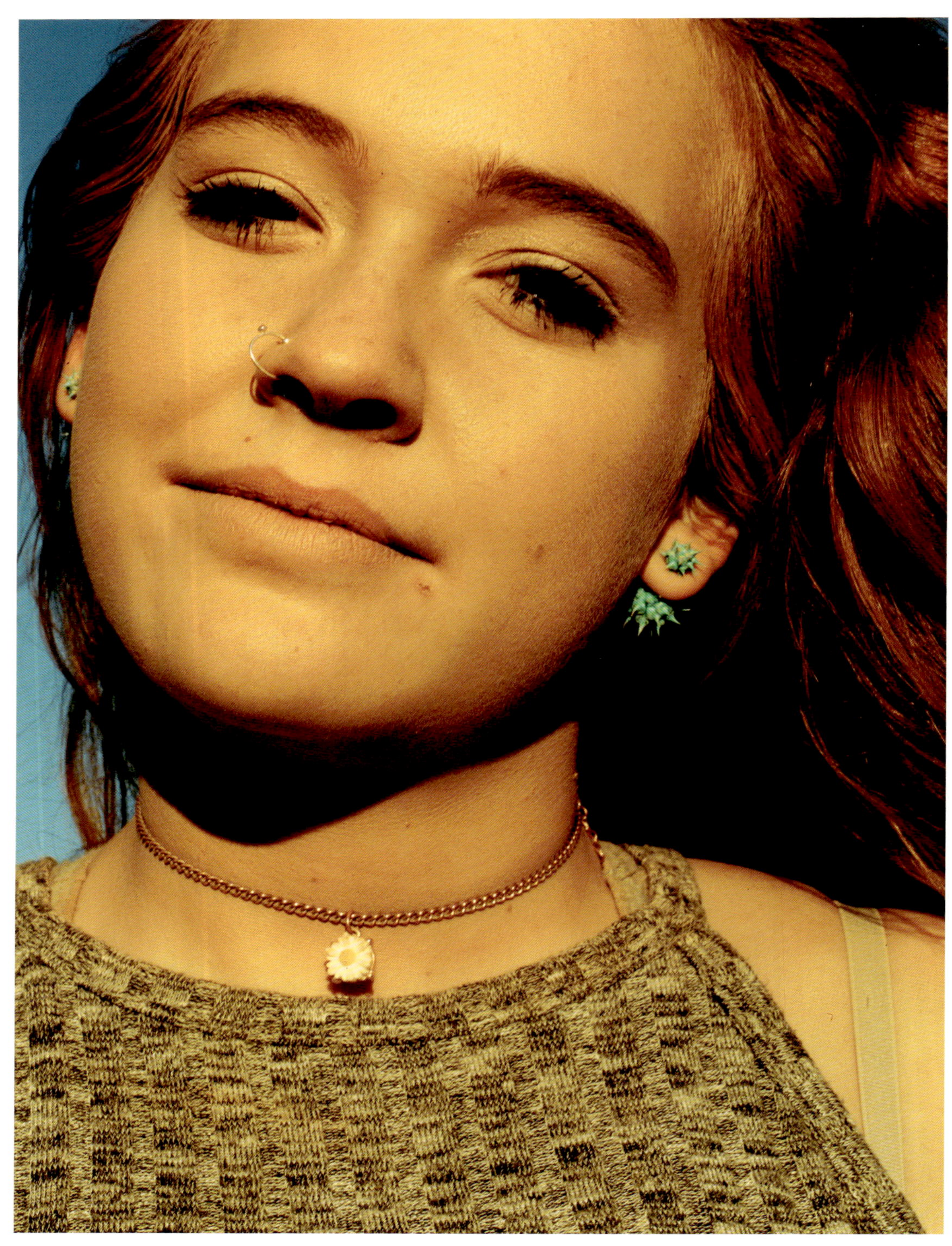

Sunset audience. Tasmania

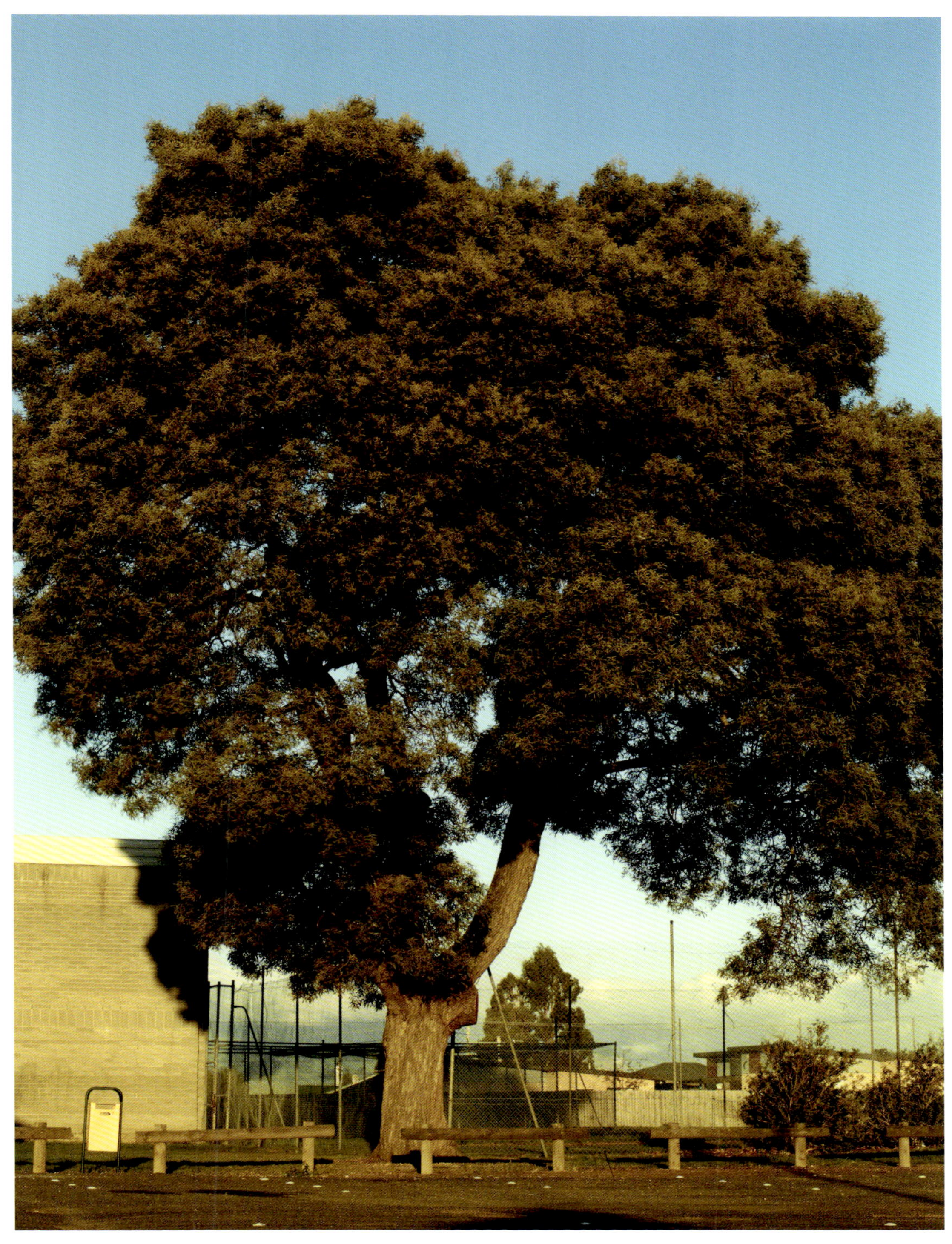

Sunset tree. Tasmania

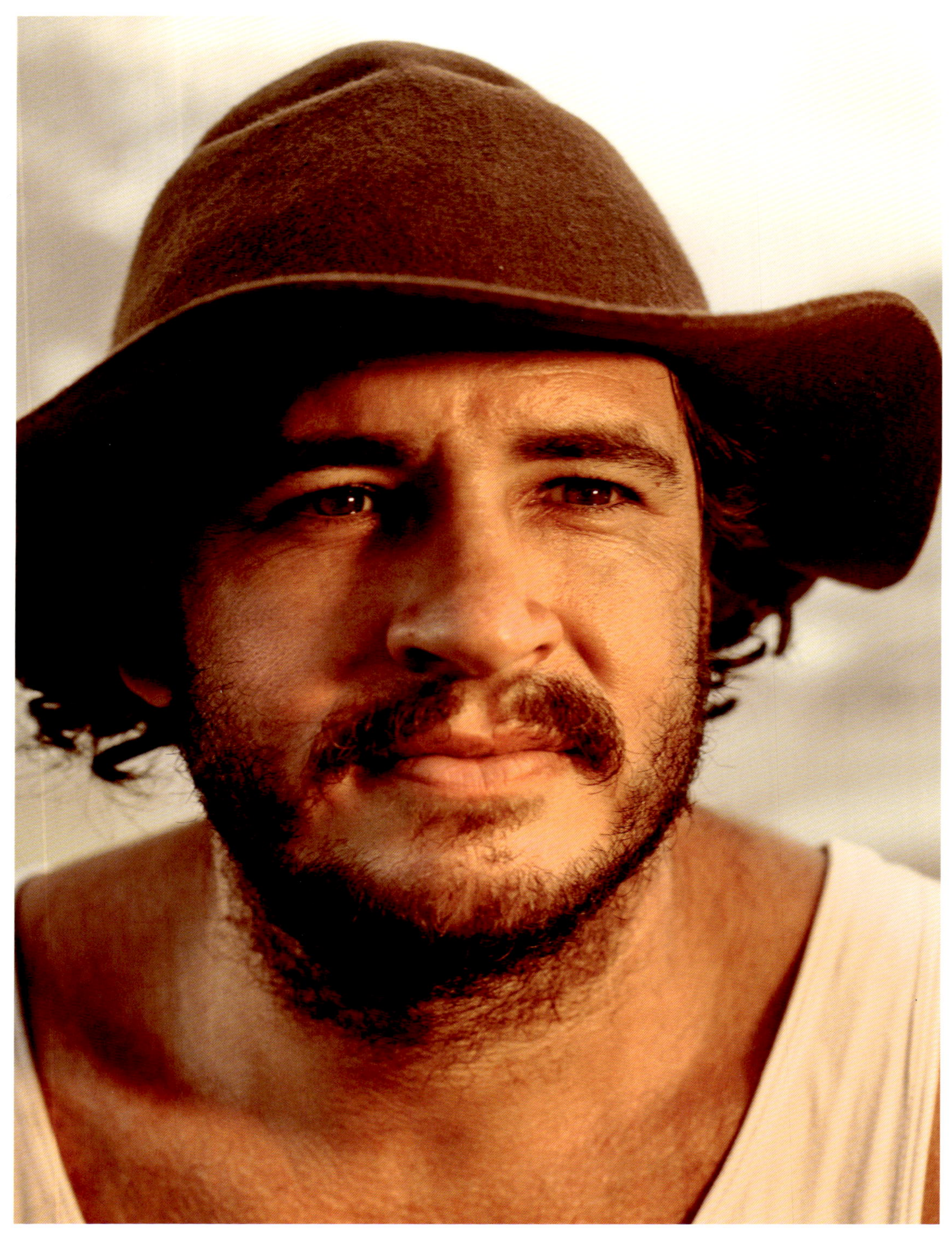

Smokey. Brunswick Heads

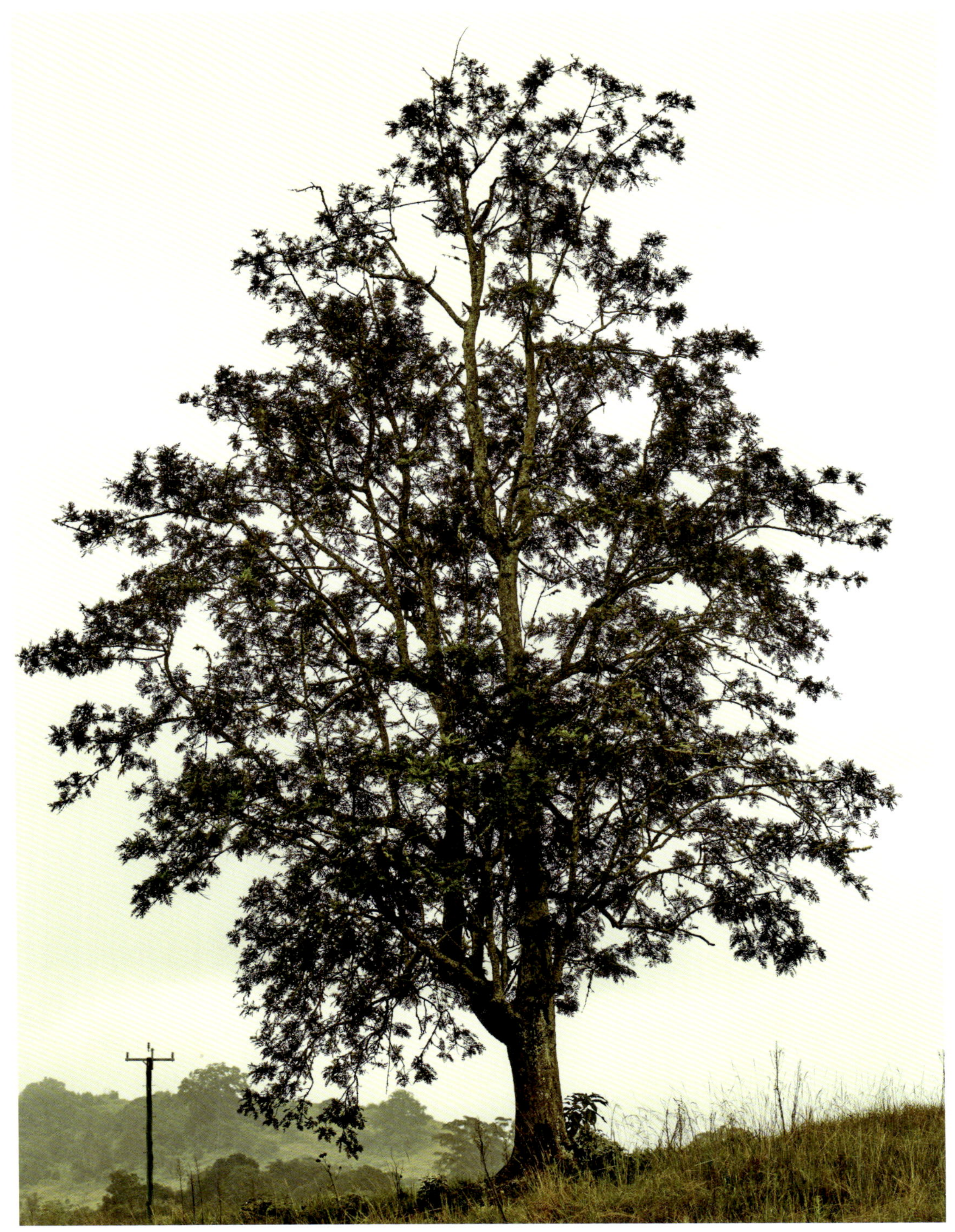

Bjorn's Tree. Byron Bay

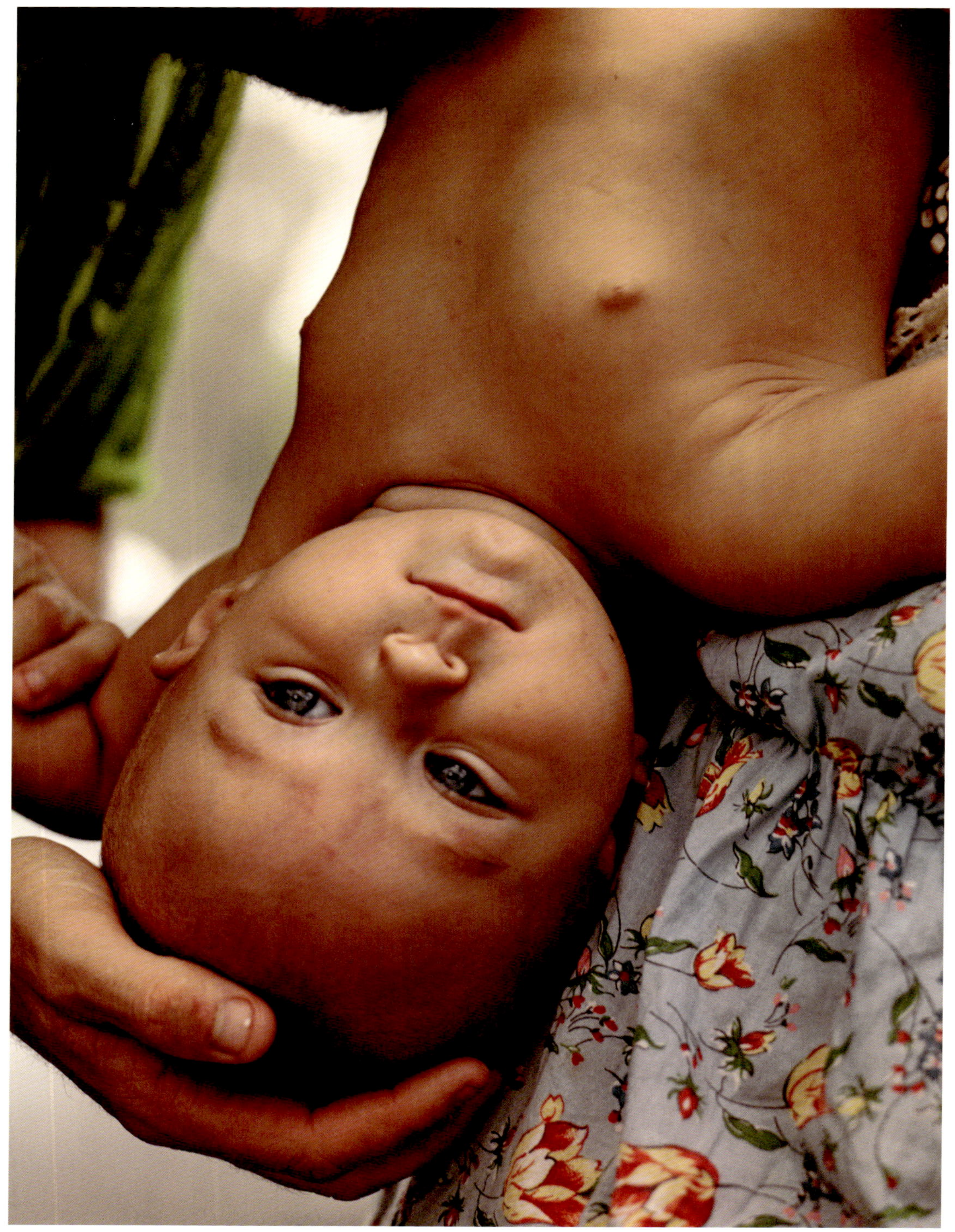

Dove. Mullum

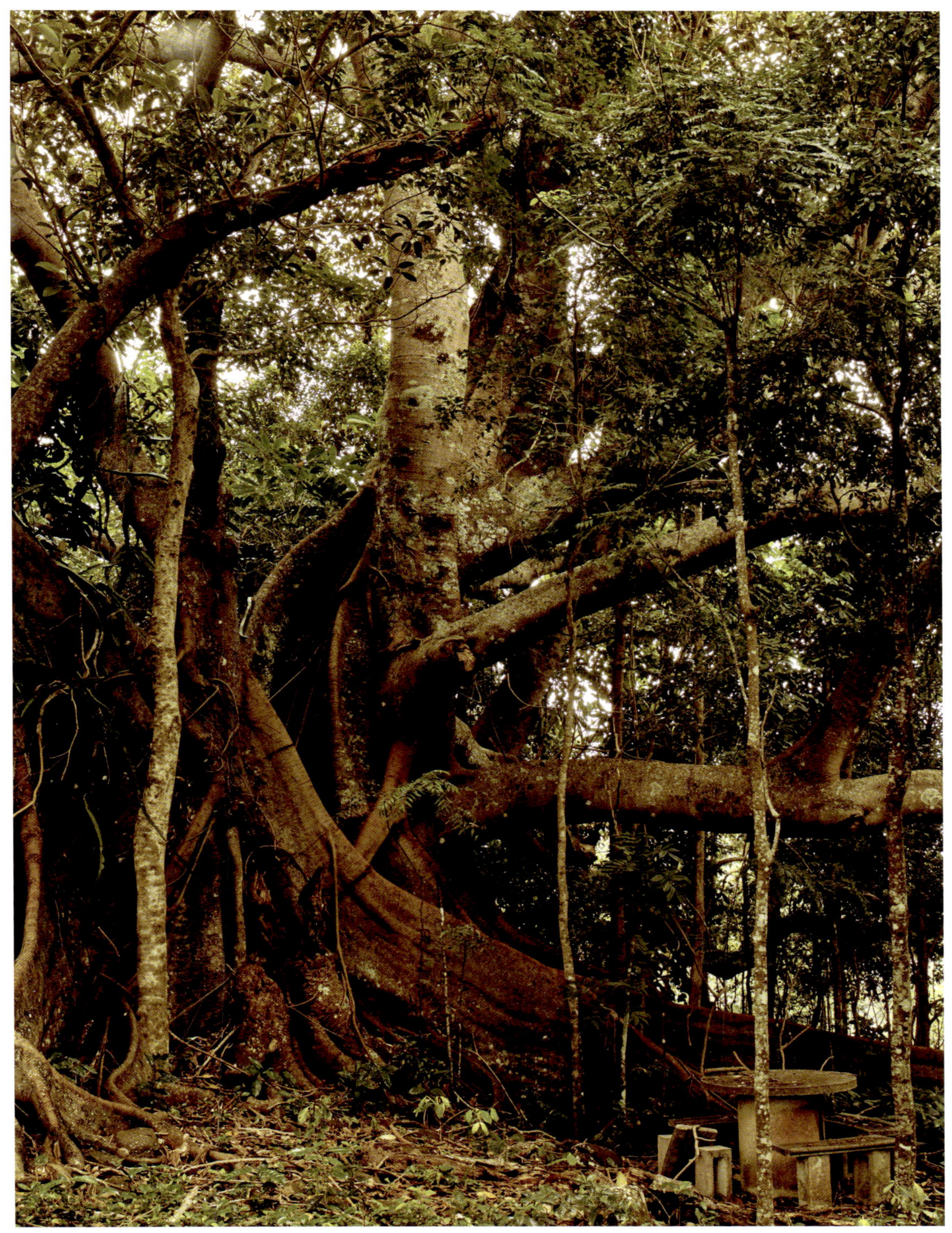

Lunch table. Whian Whian

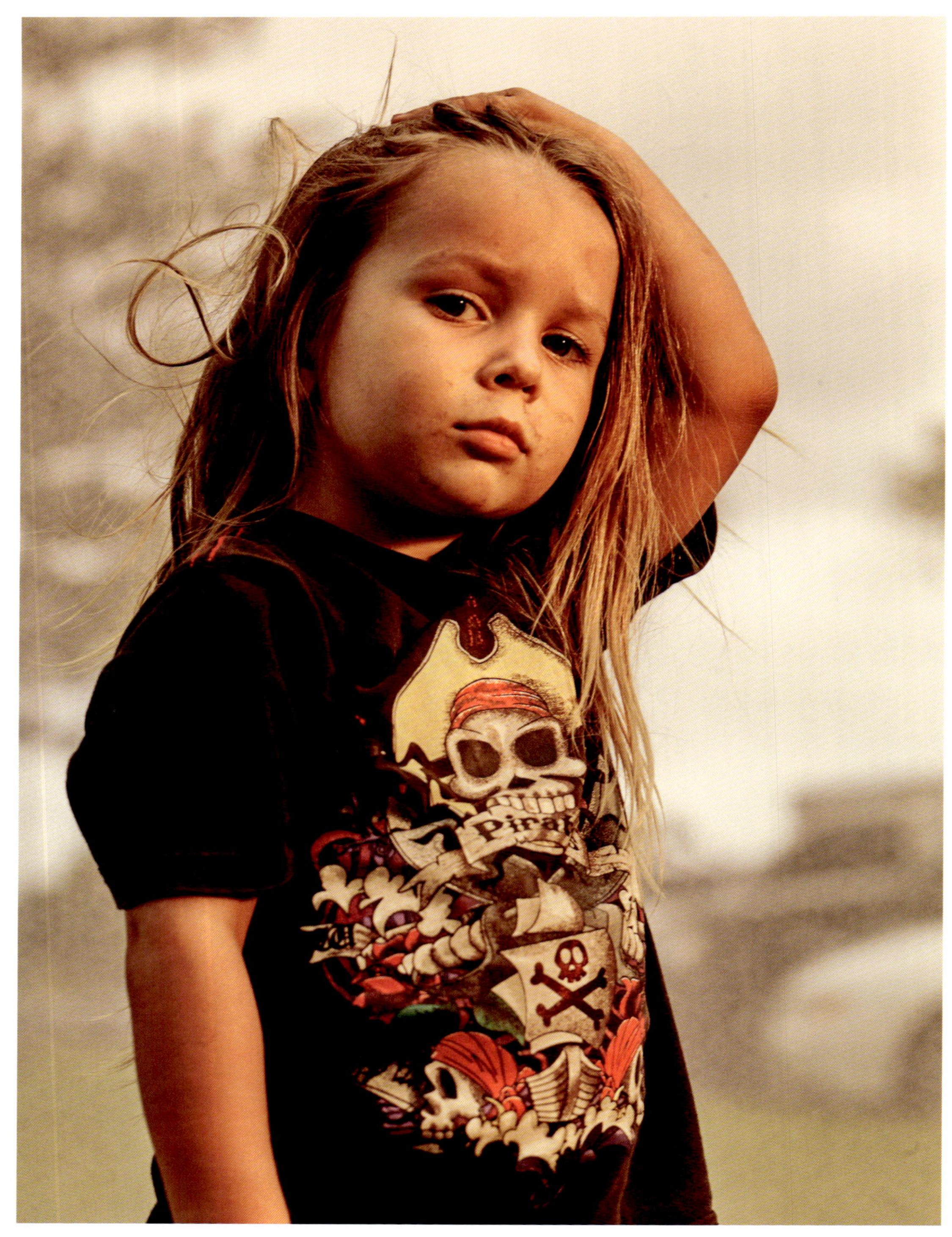

Neo. Brunwick Heads

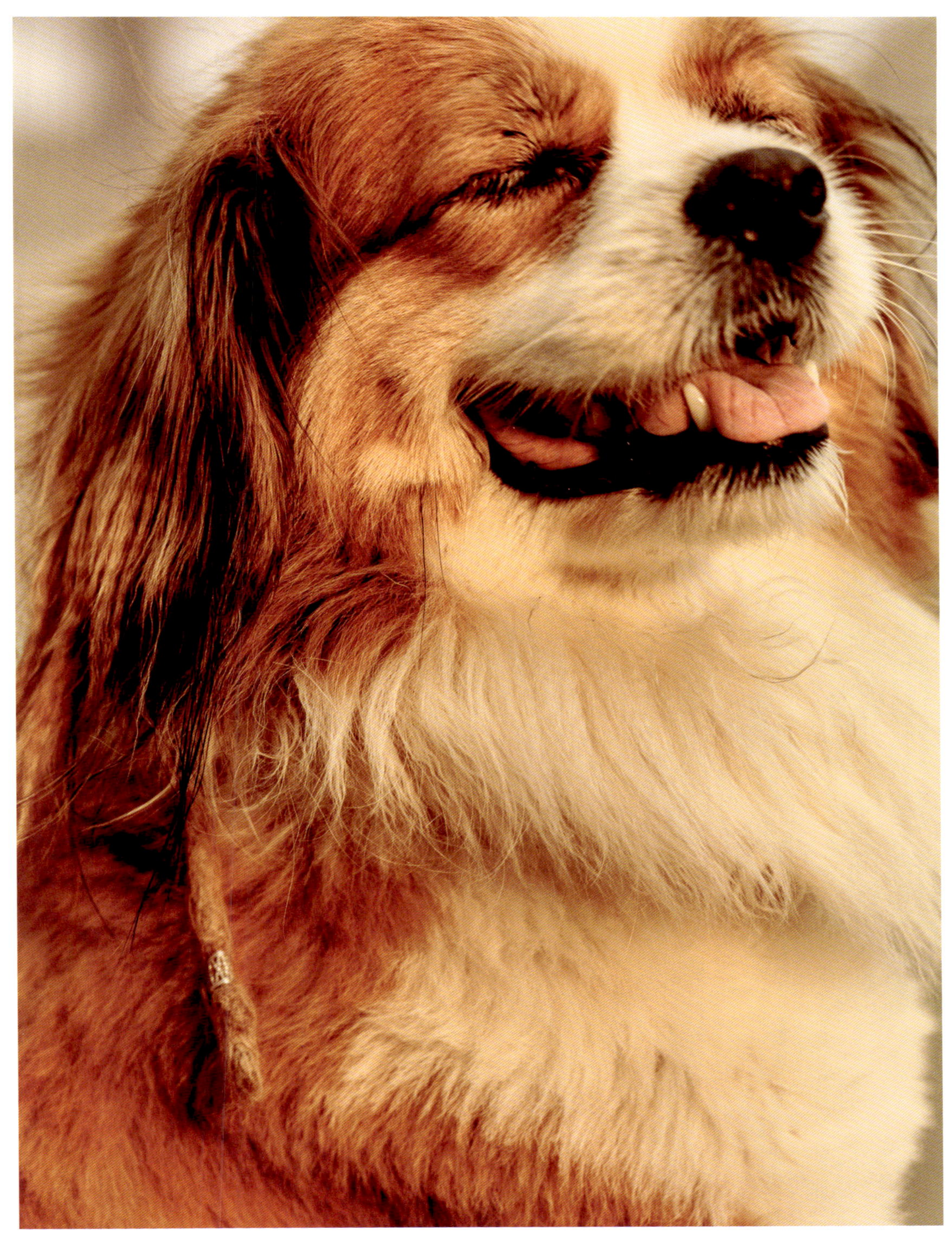

Stoner Dog. Brunswick Heads

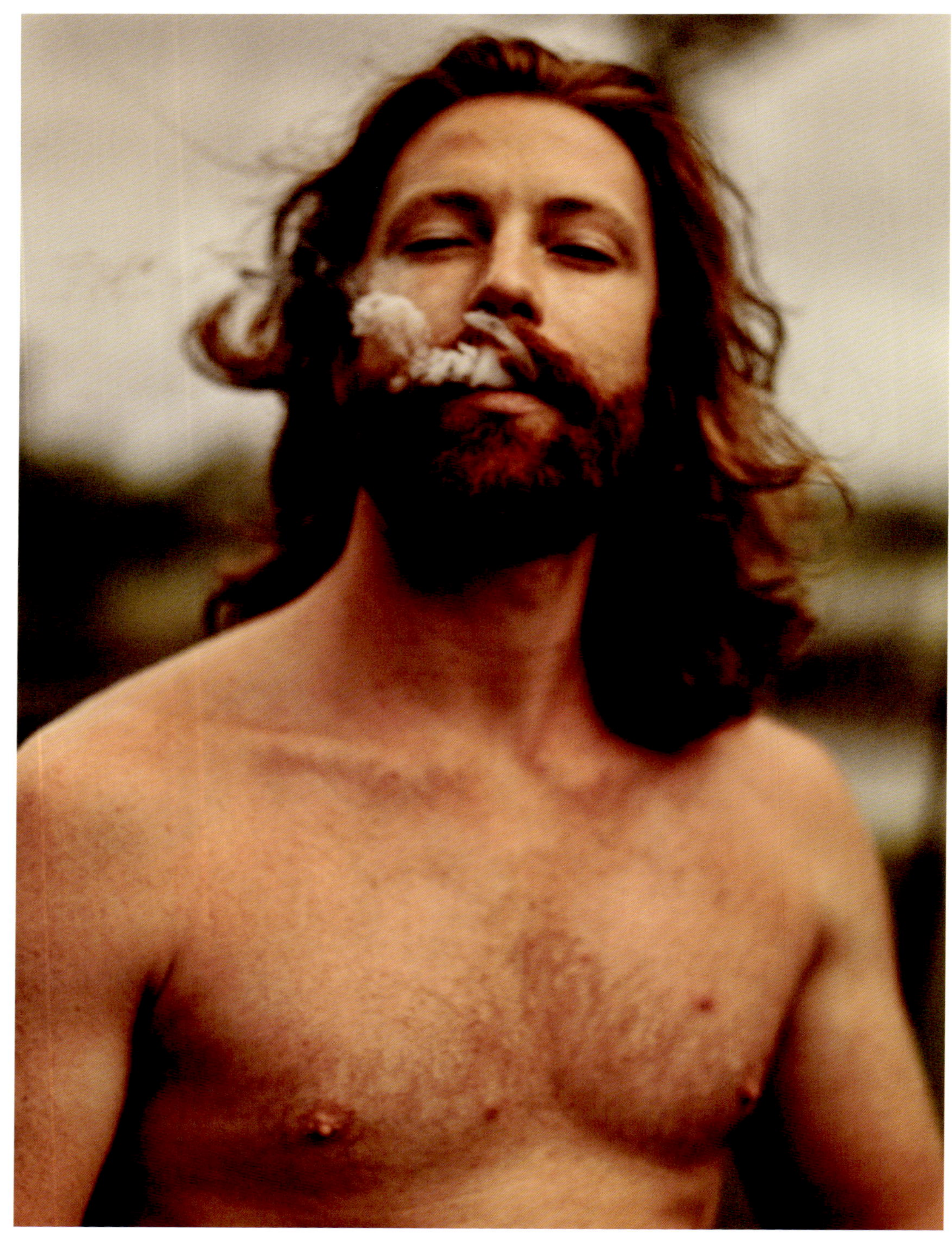

Rob. North Coast

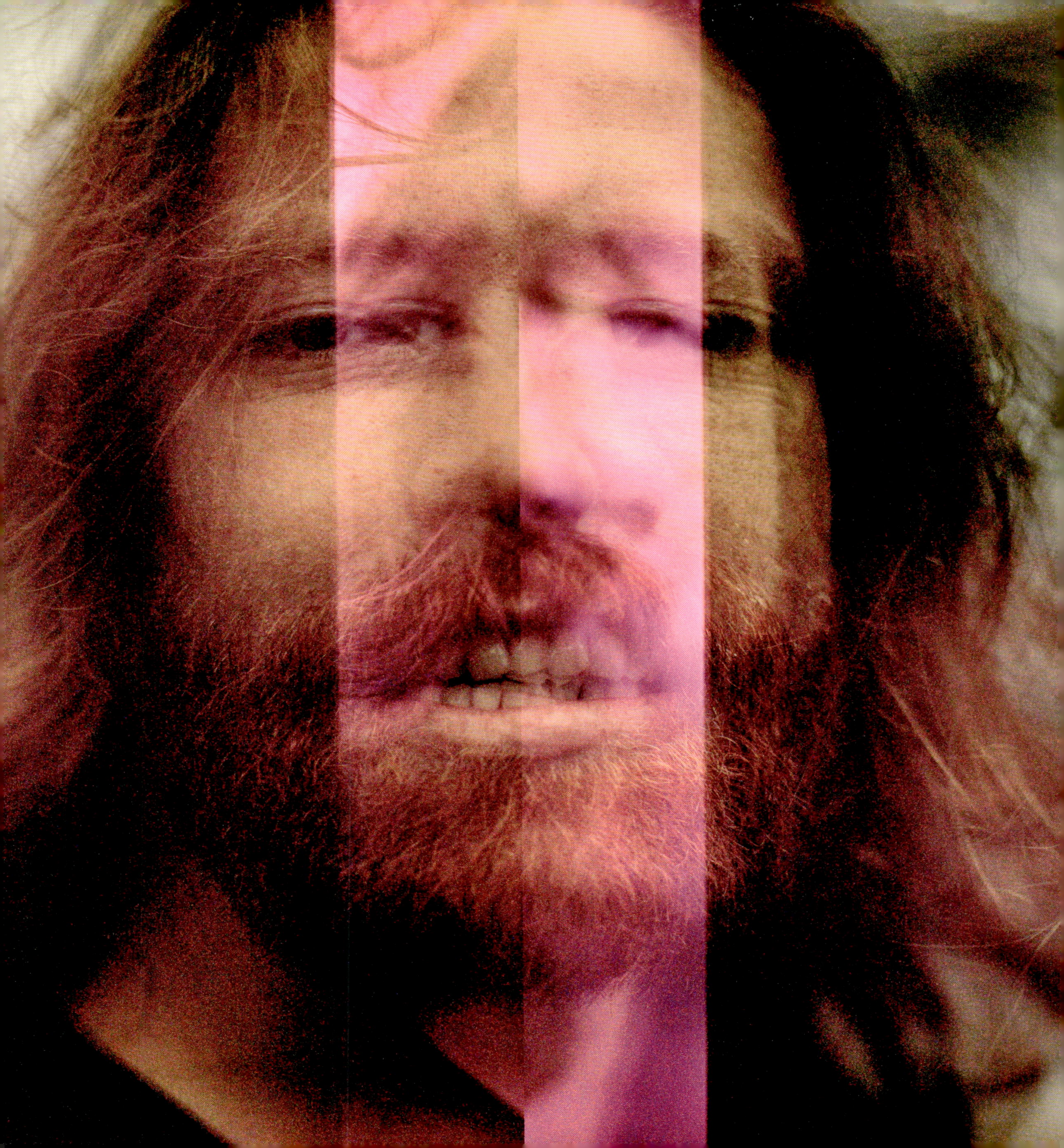

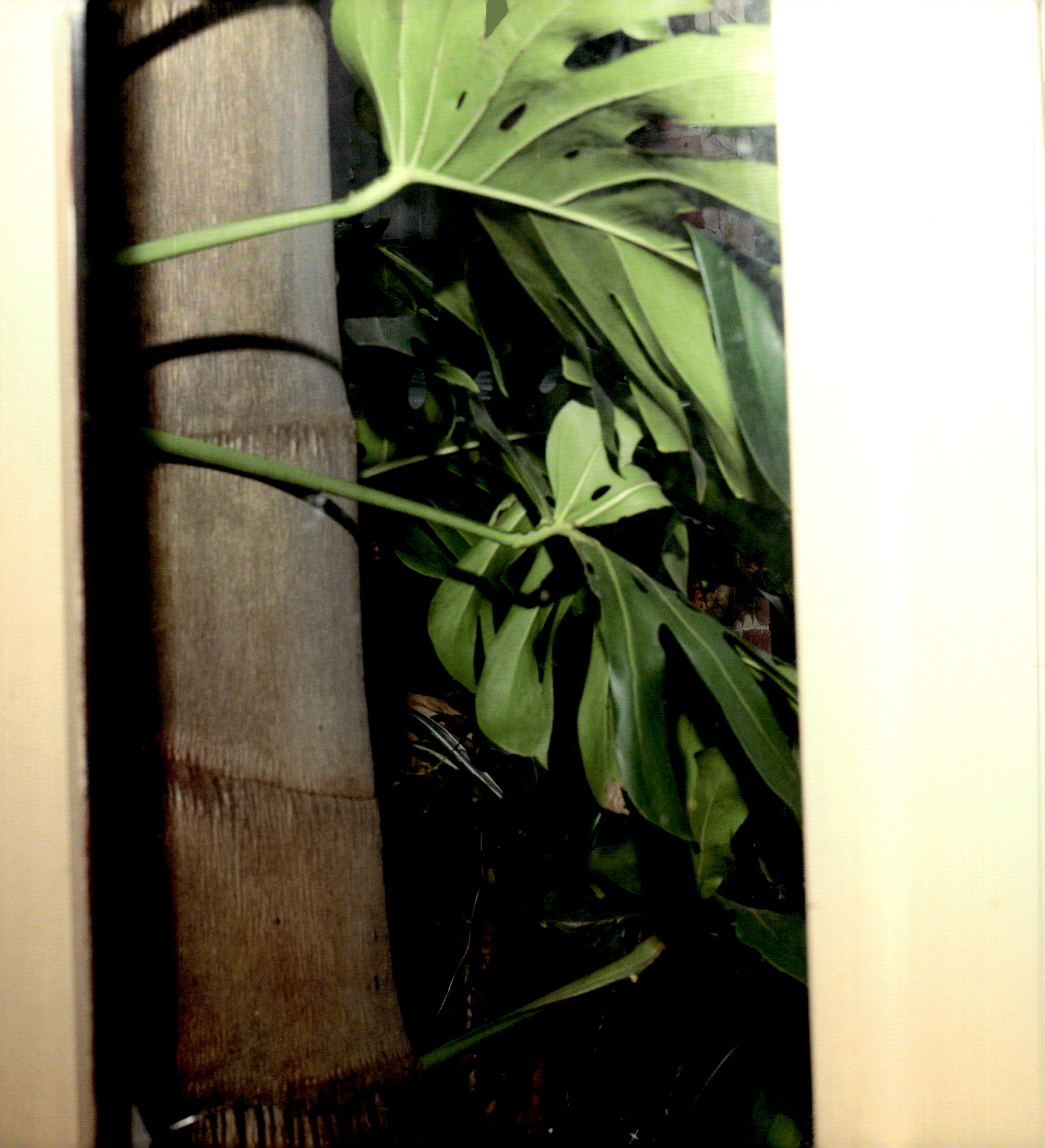

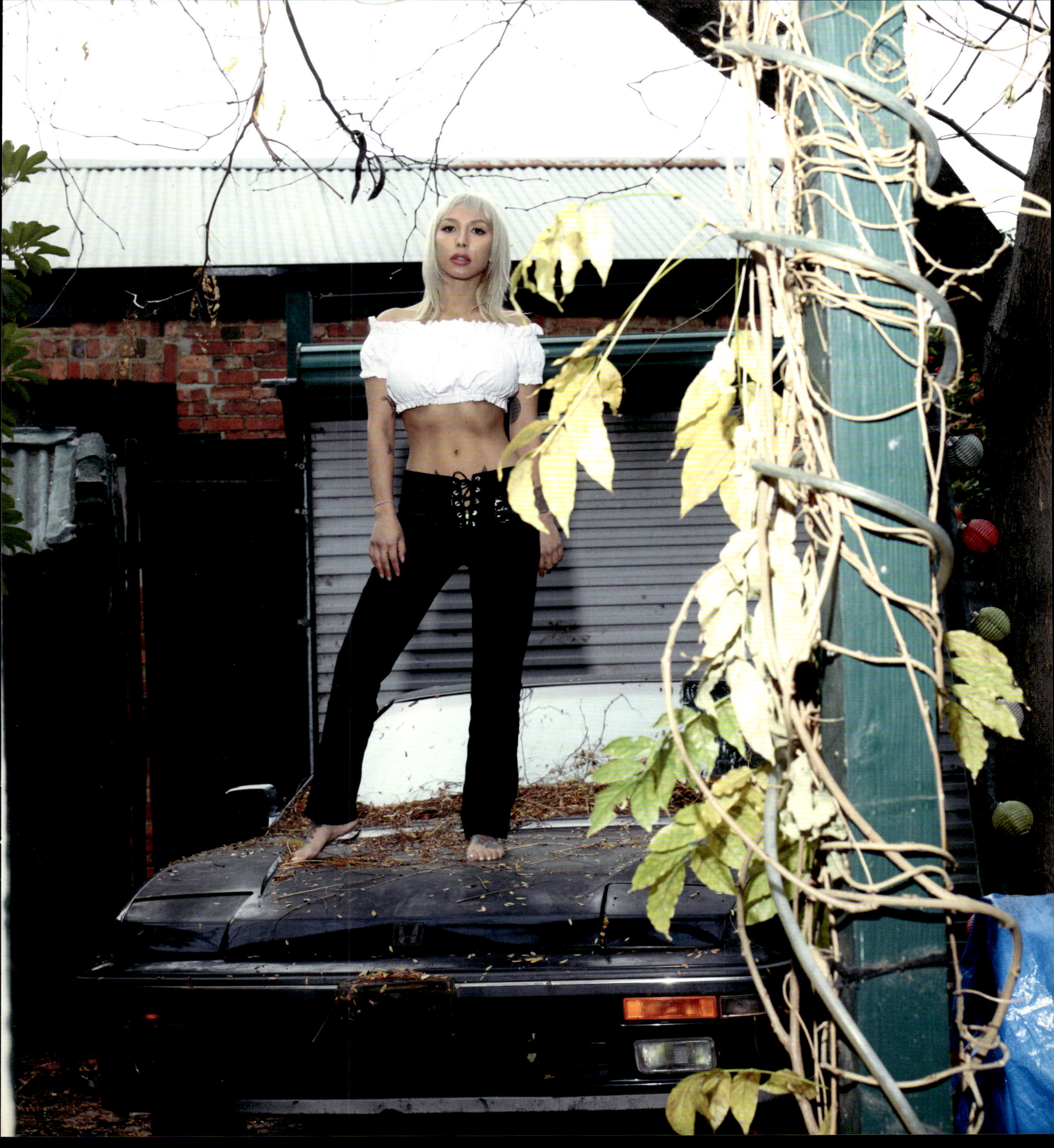

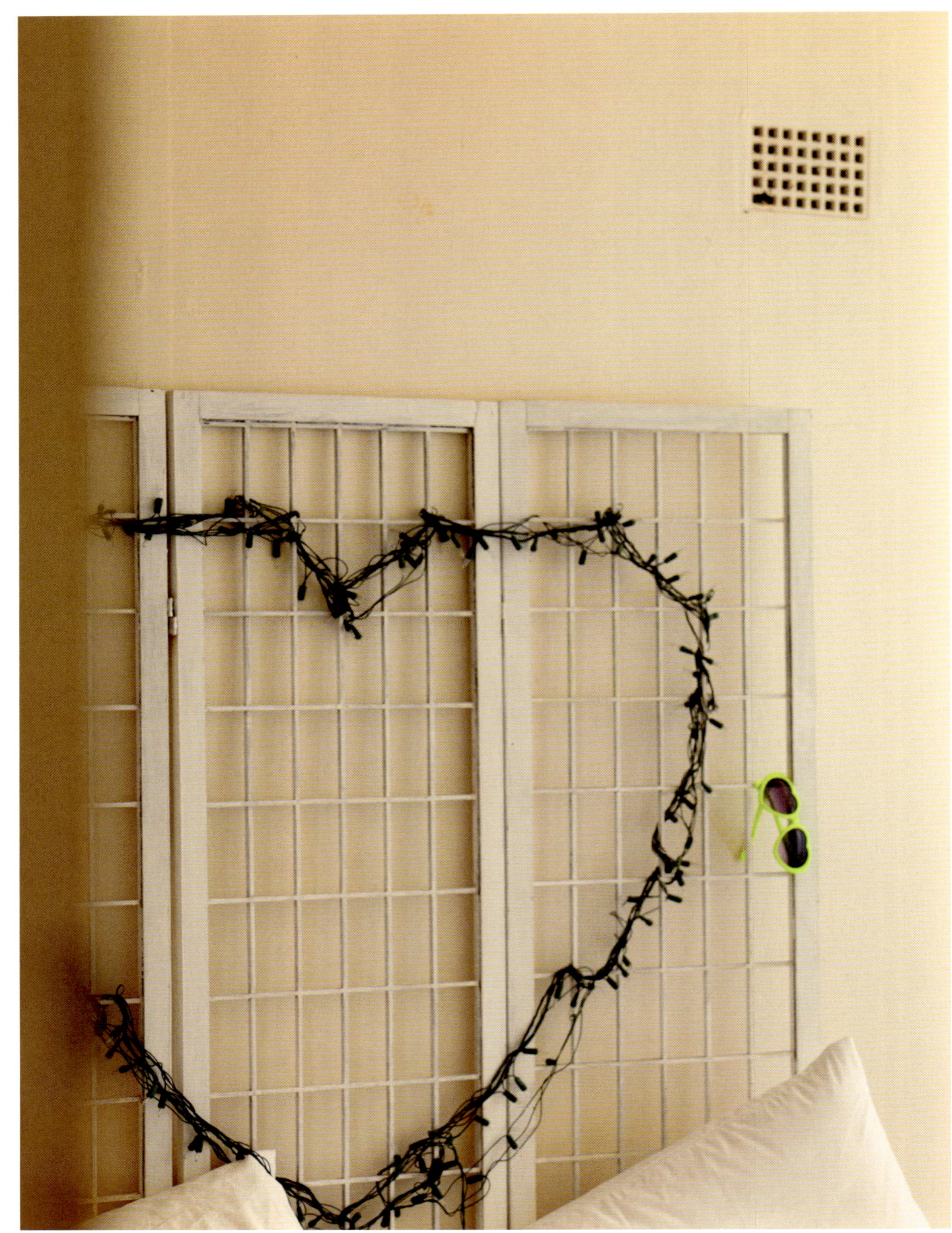

Claire's Bed Head. Bondi

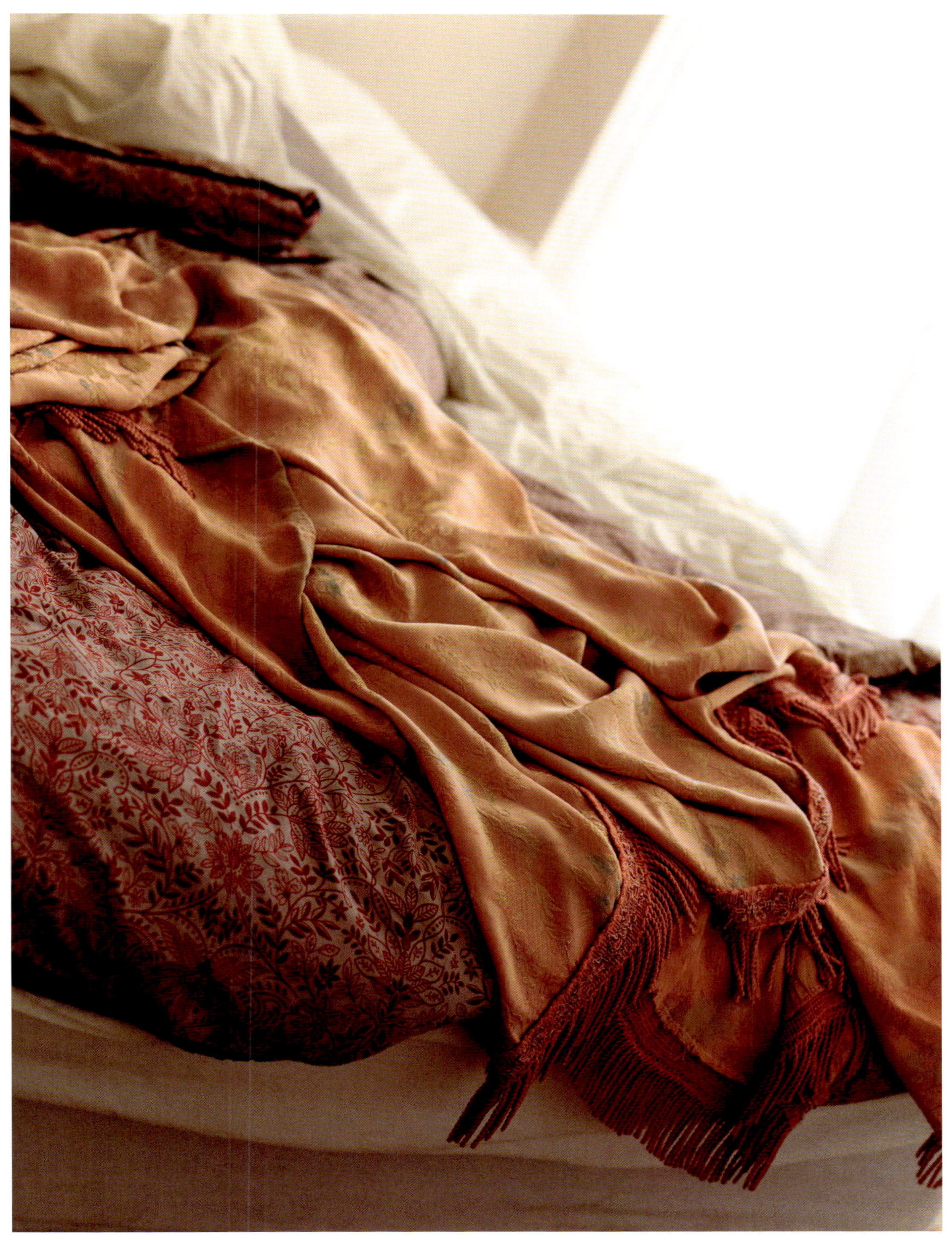

Claire's Blanket. Bondi

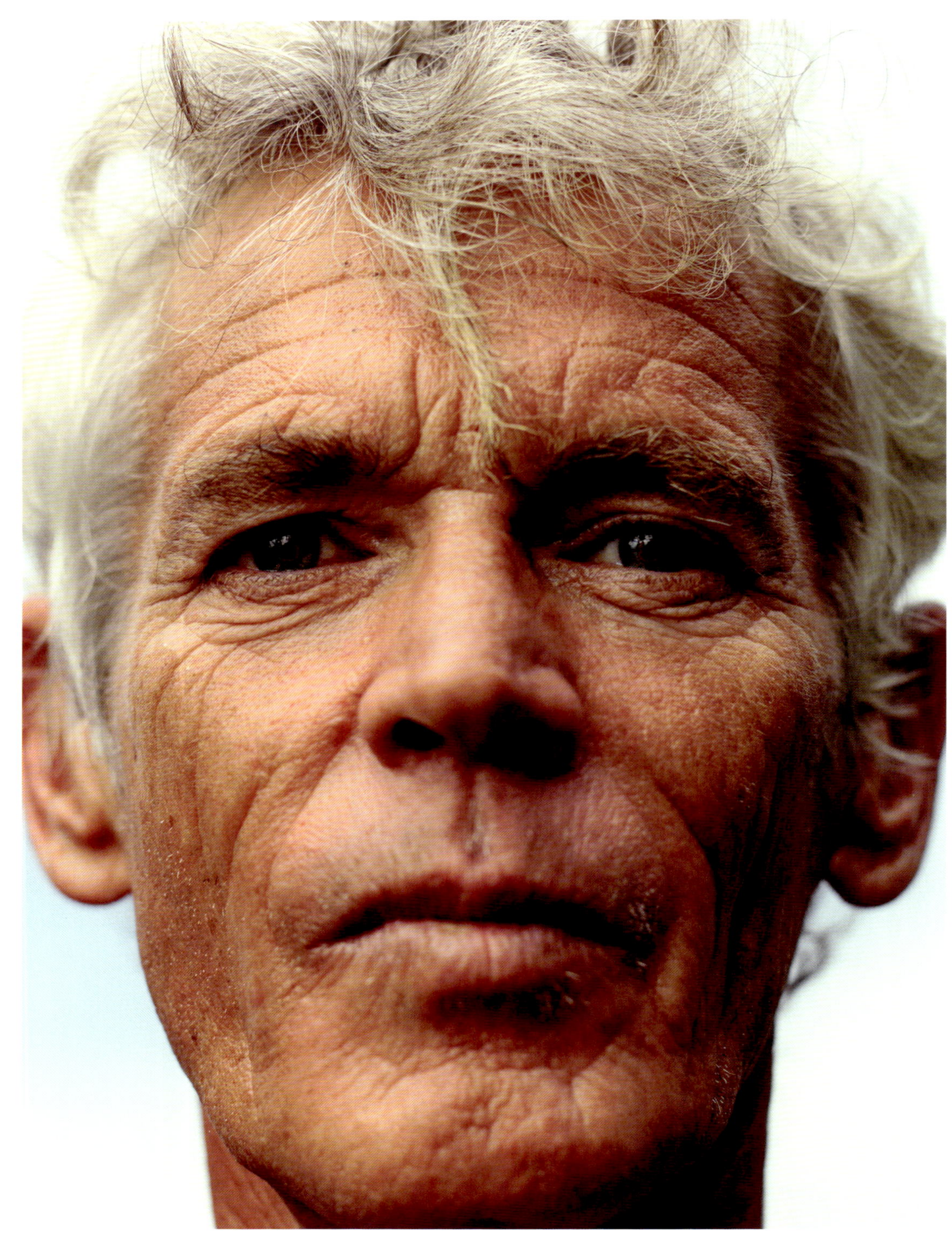

Paul. Gold Coast

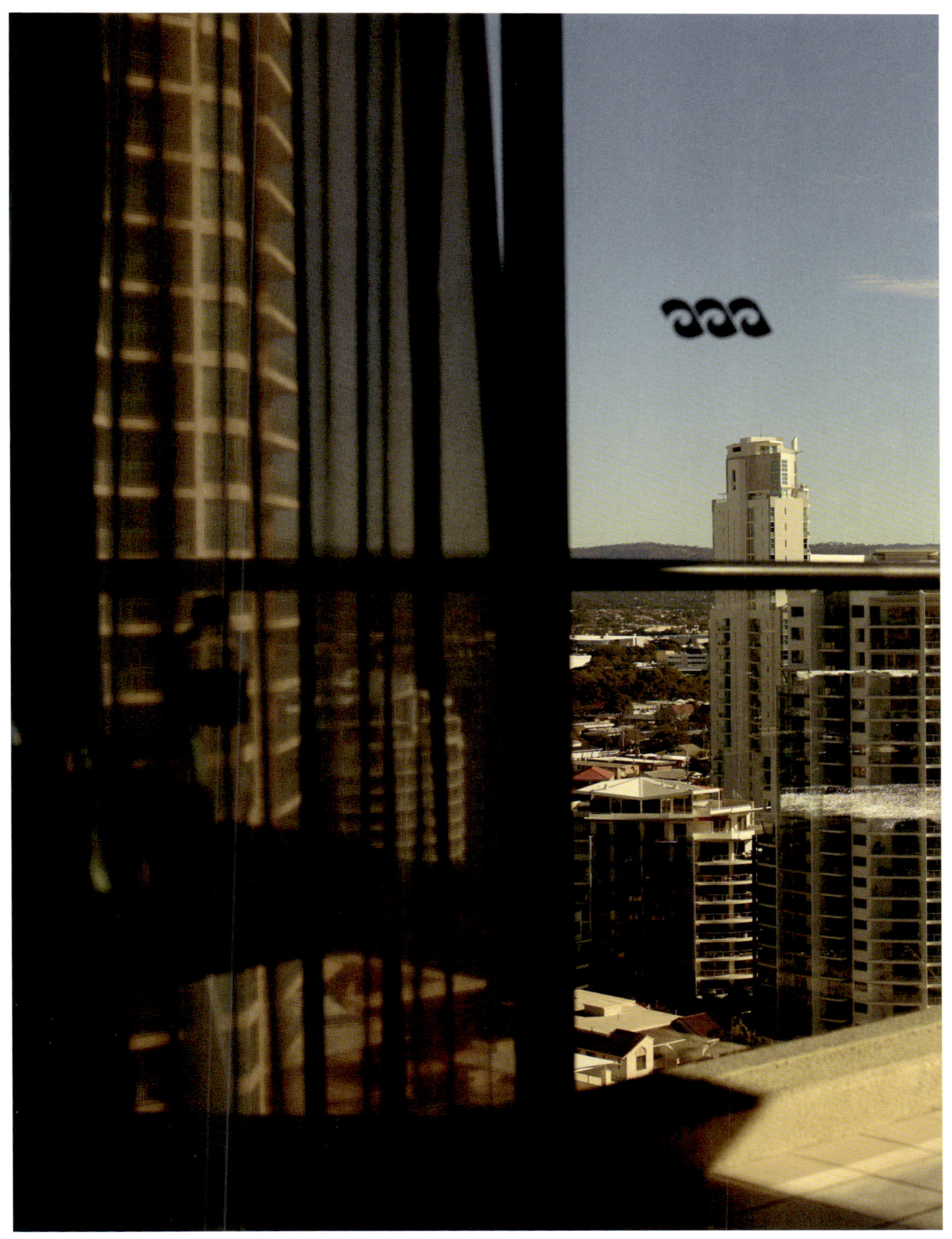

My hotel. Gold Coast

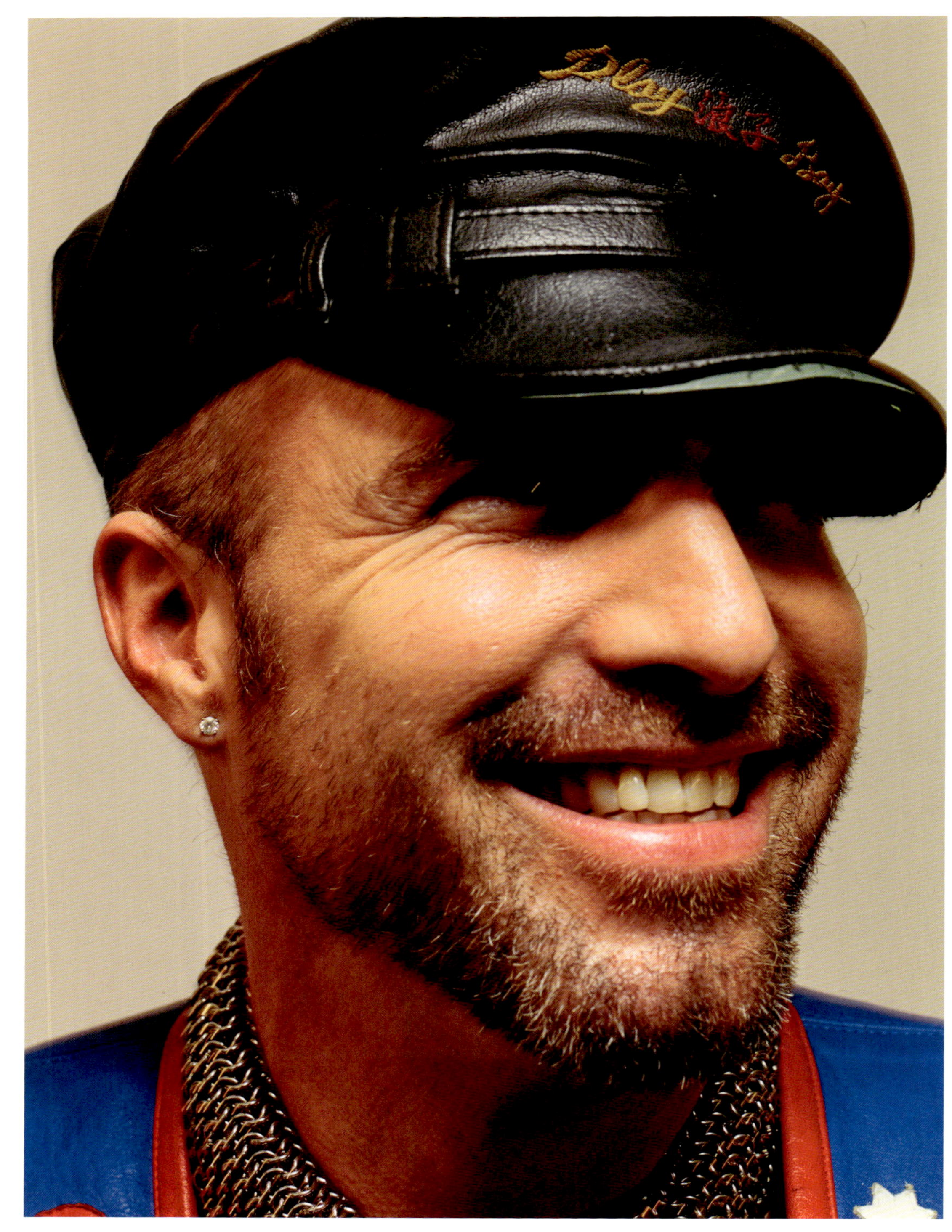

Mr Leather. Redhill

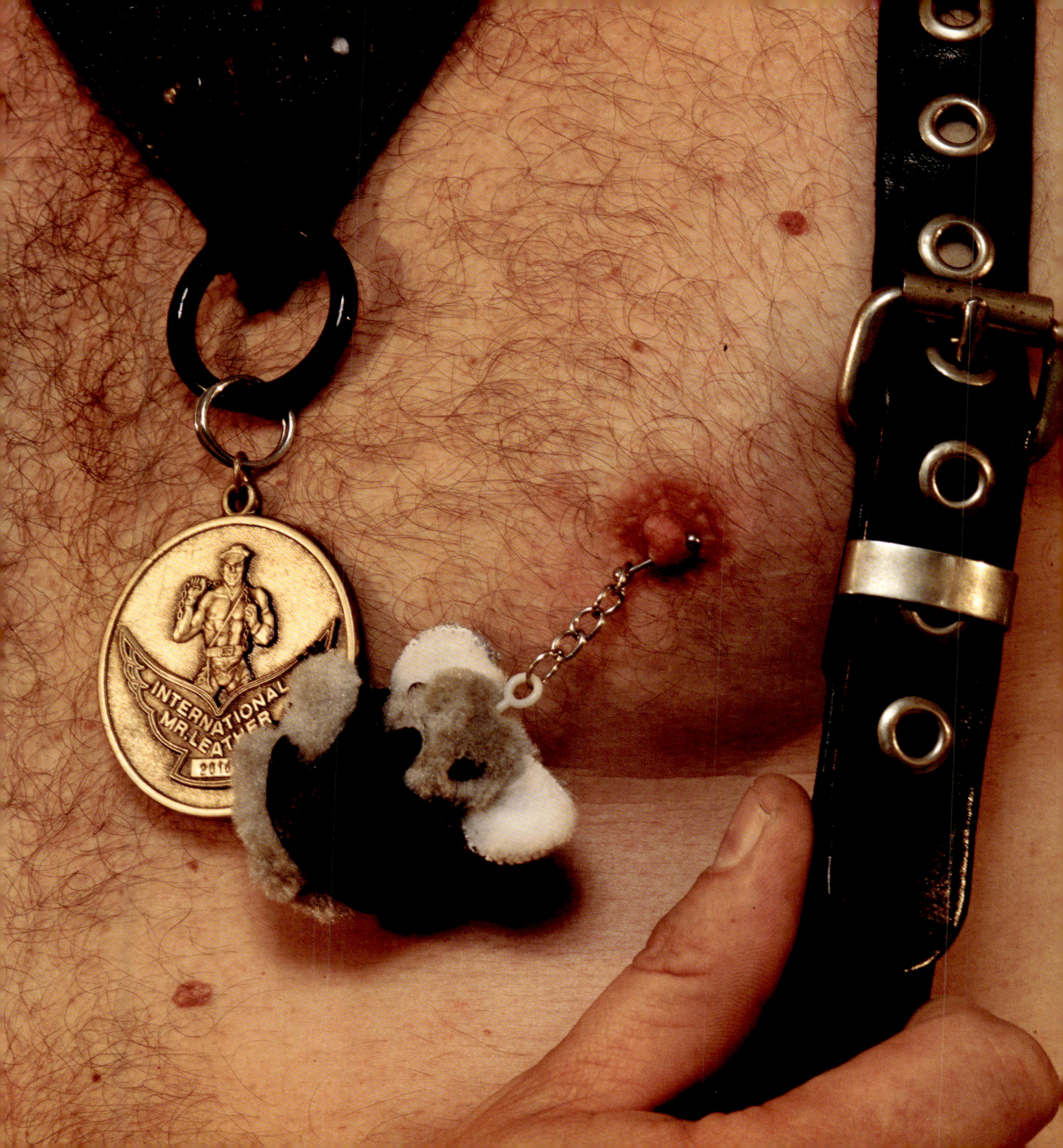

INTERNATIONAL
MR. LEATHER
2016

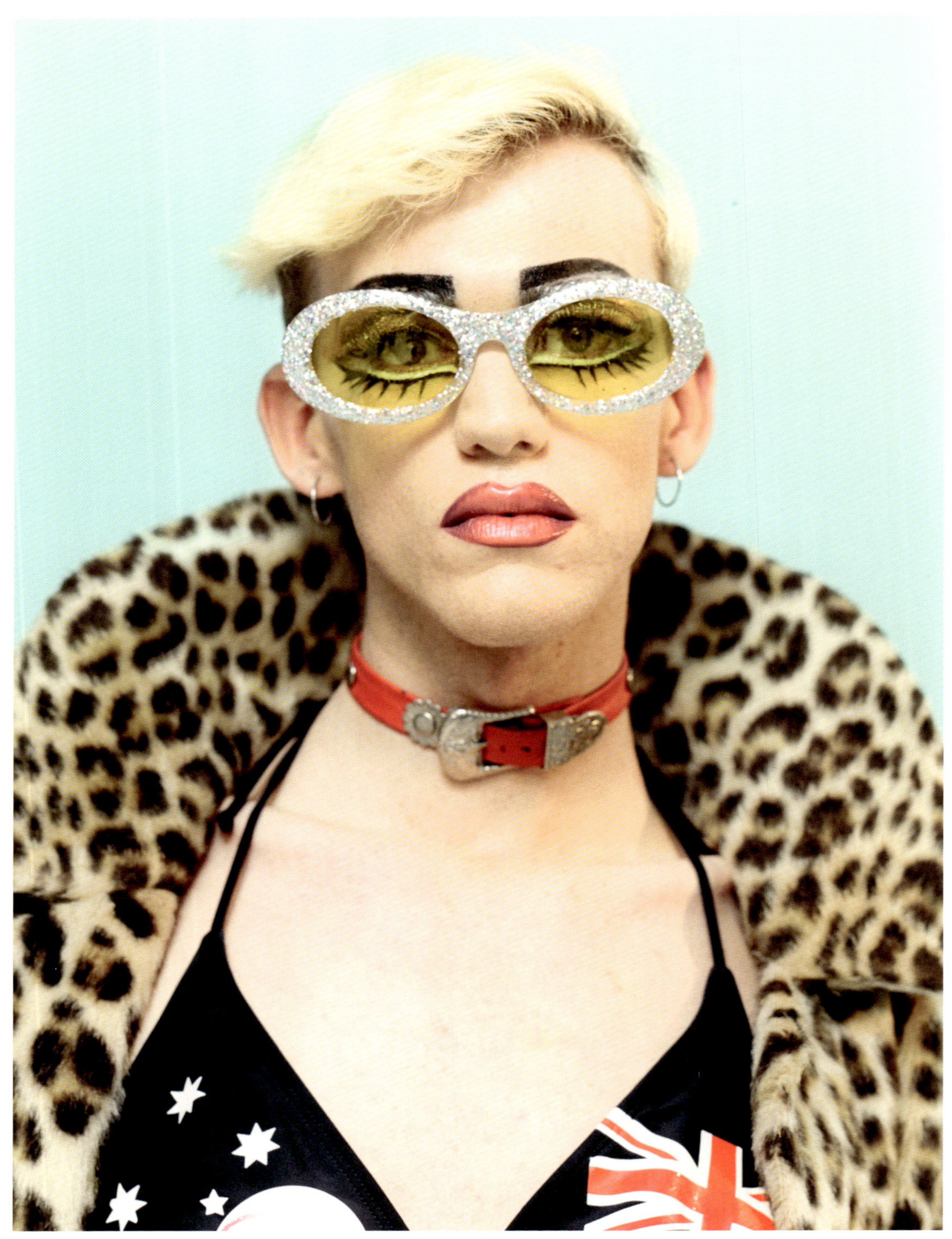

Starky Shake. Sydney

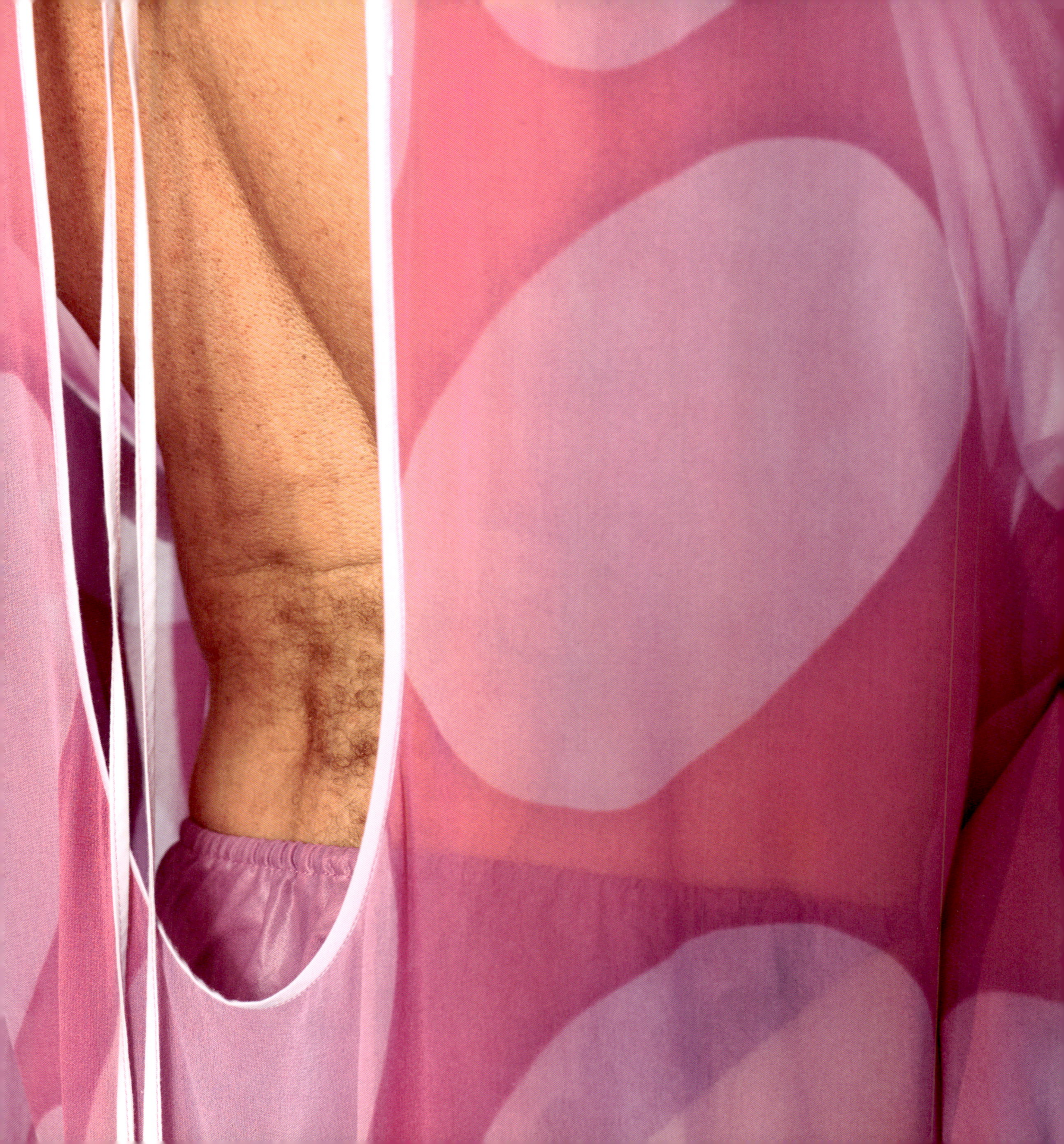

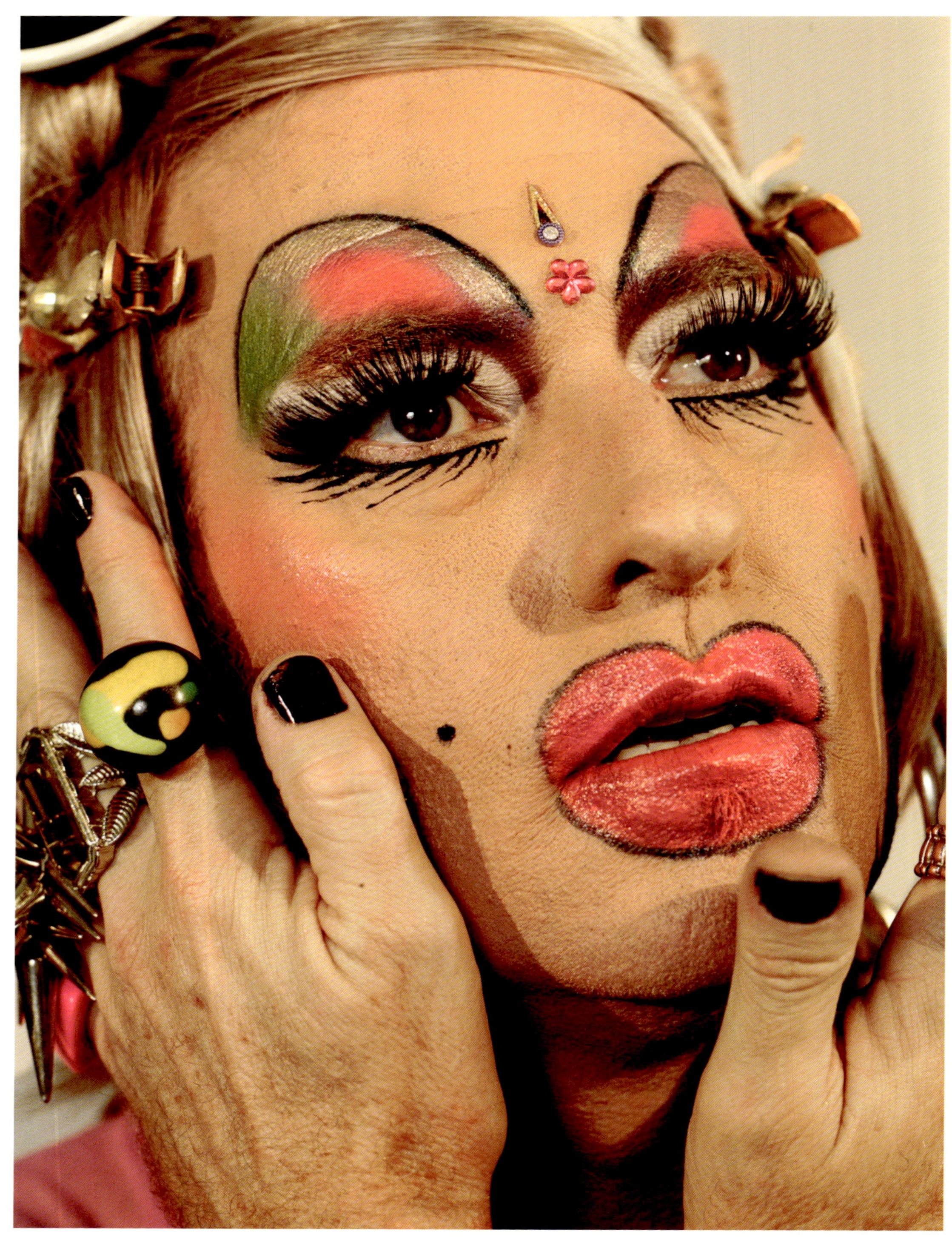

Vanessa Wagner. Sydney

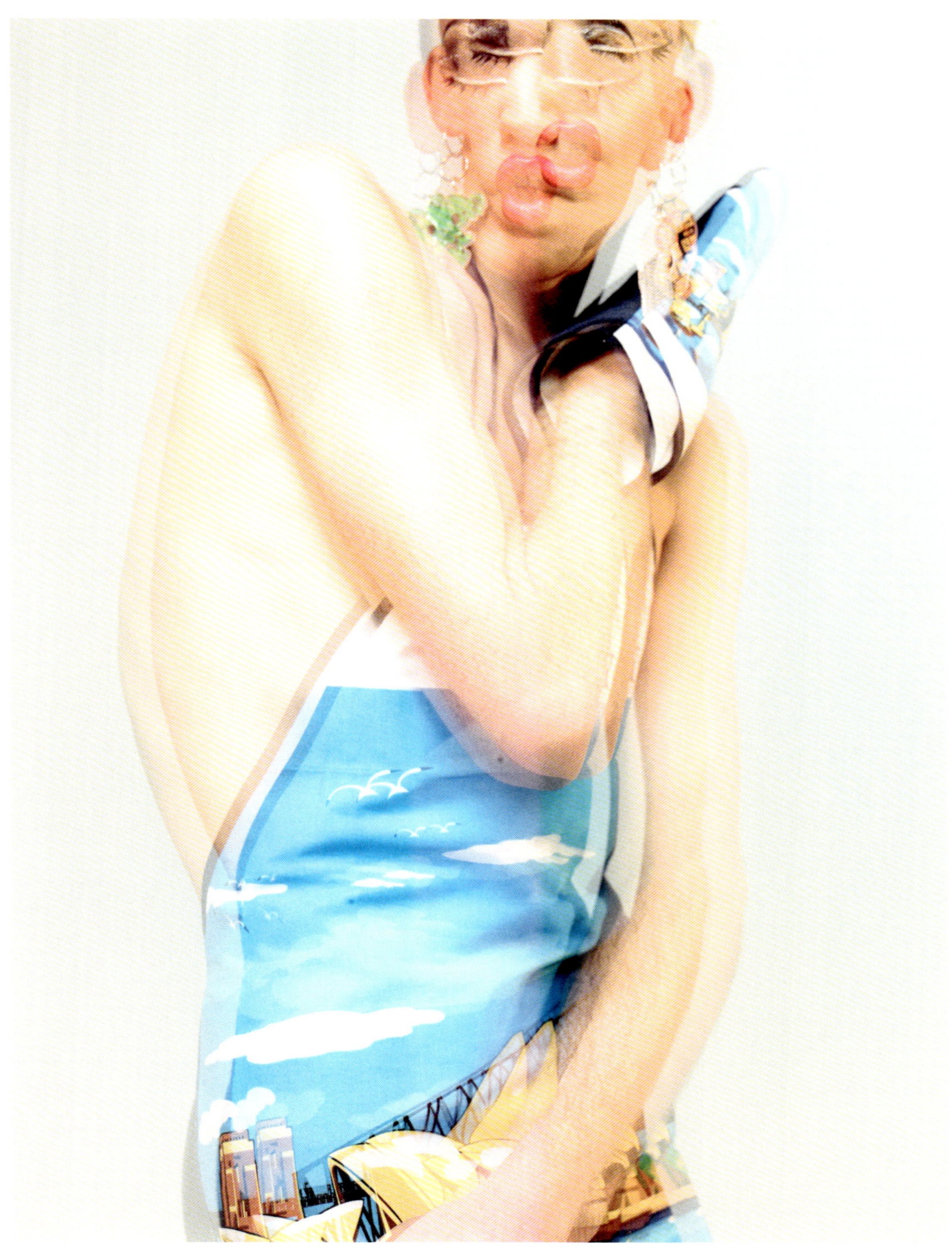

Starky Shake. Sydney

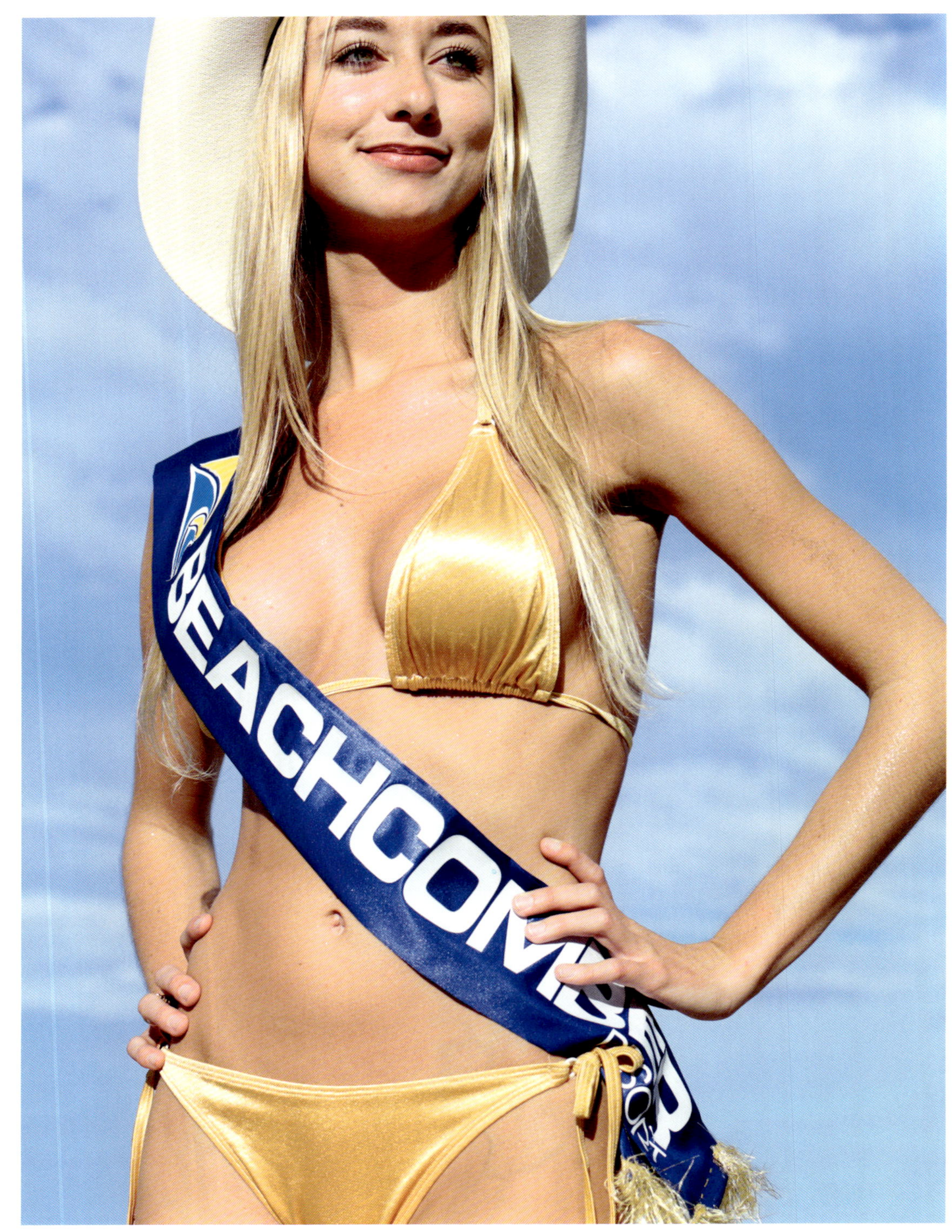

Meter Maid. Gold Coast

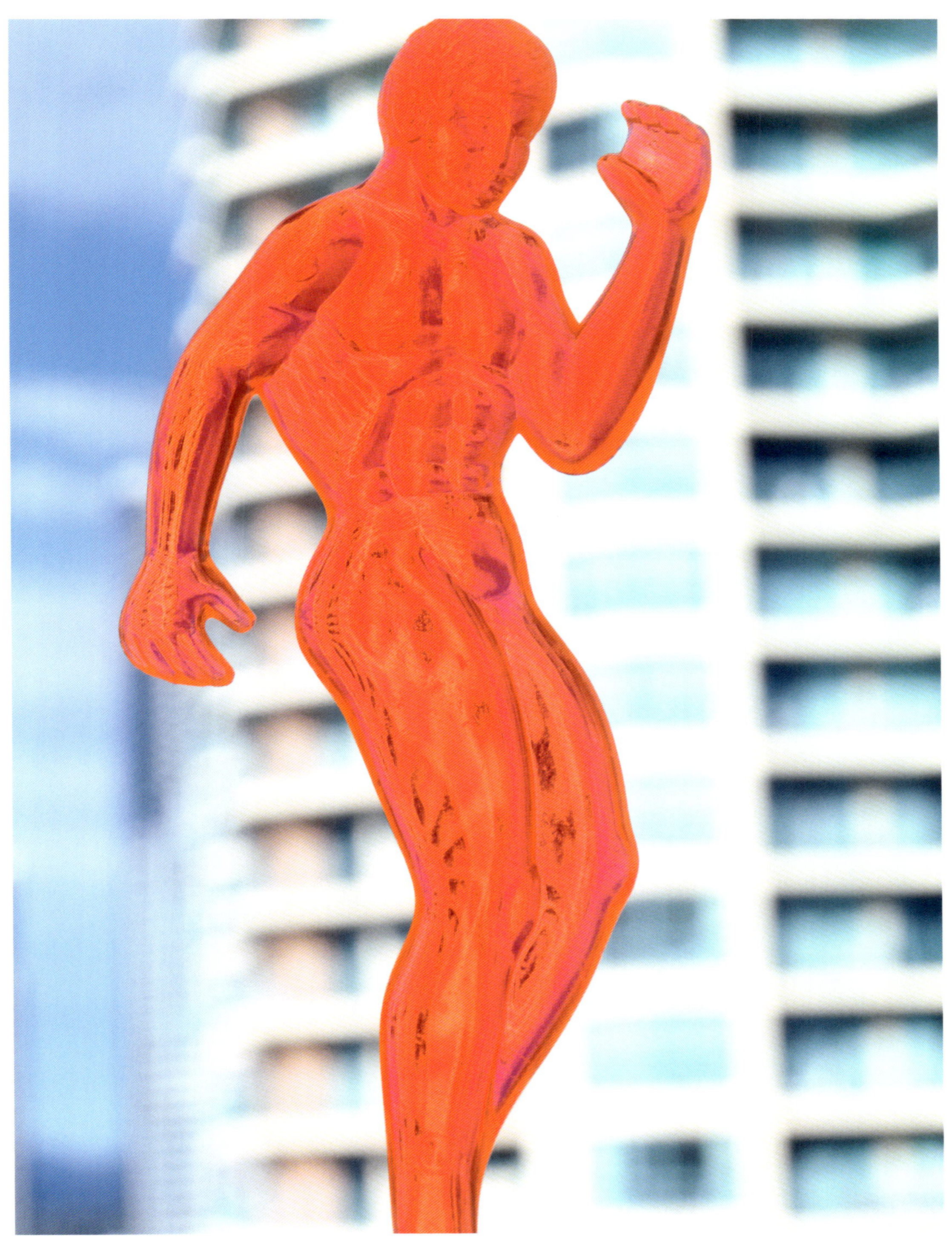

Plastic Fantastic. Gold Coast

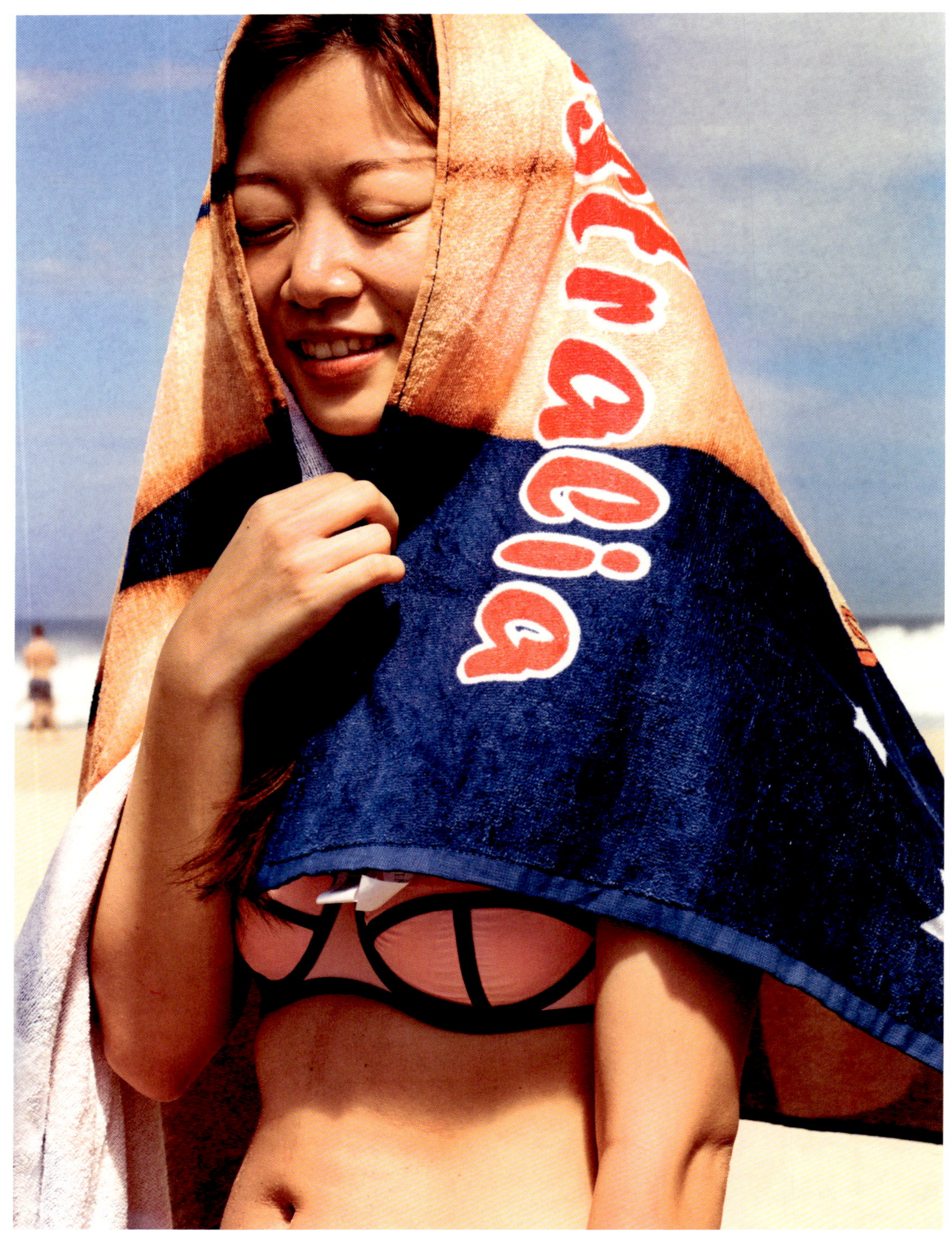

Julie. Bondi Beach

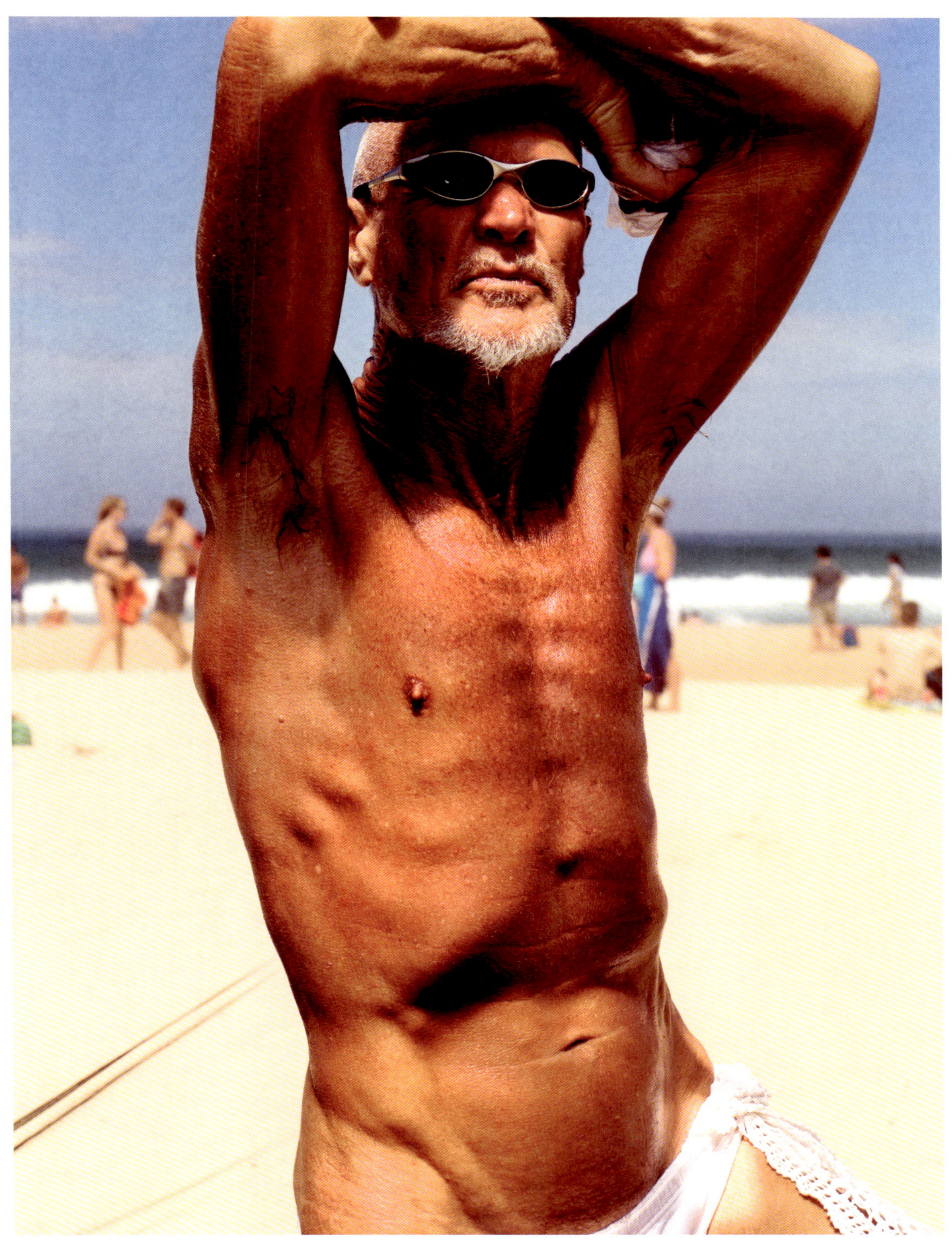

Mr. Bondi. Bondi Beach

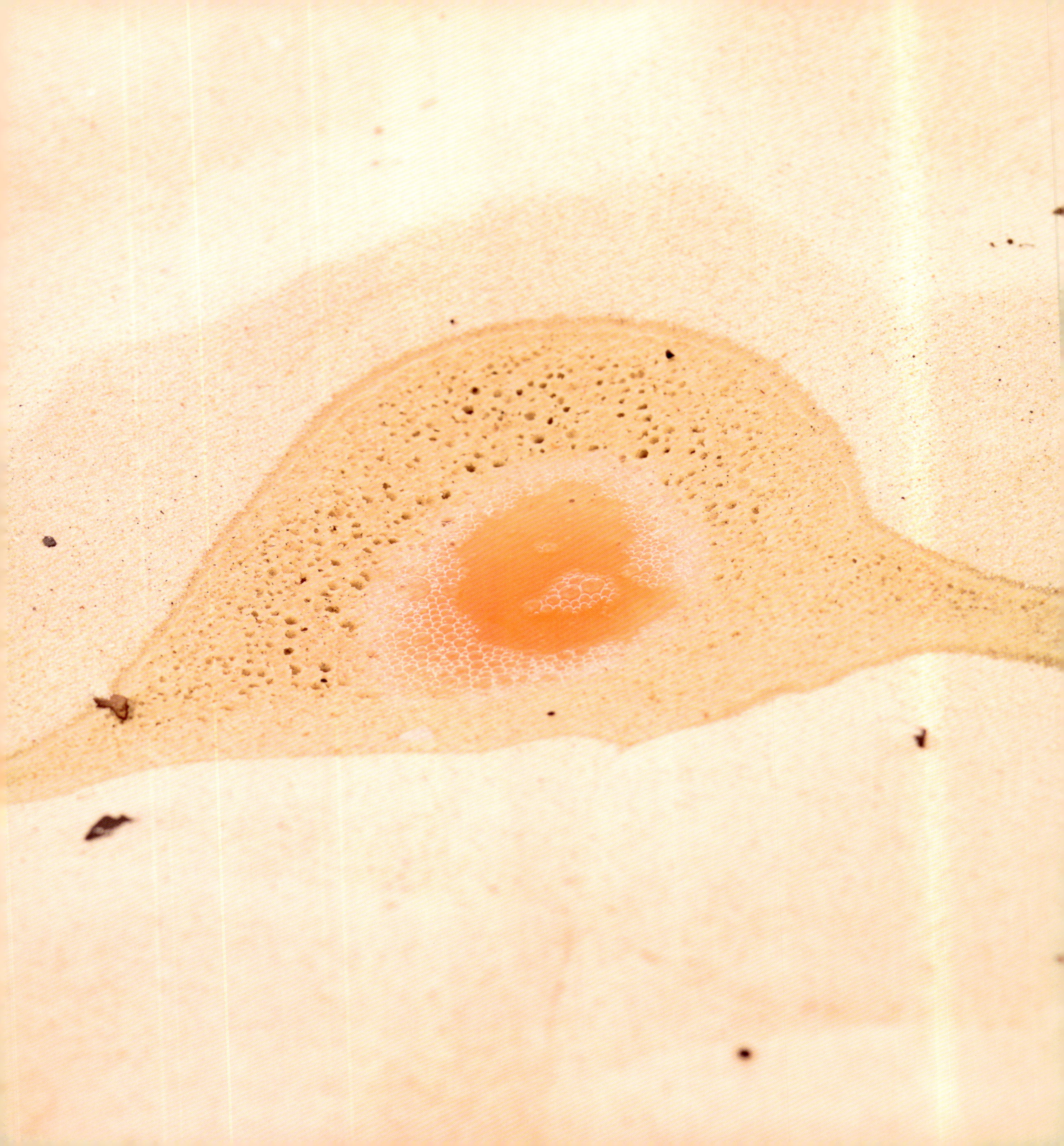

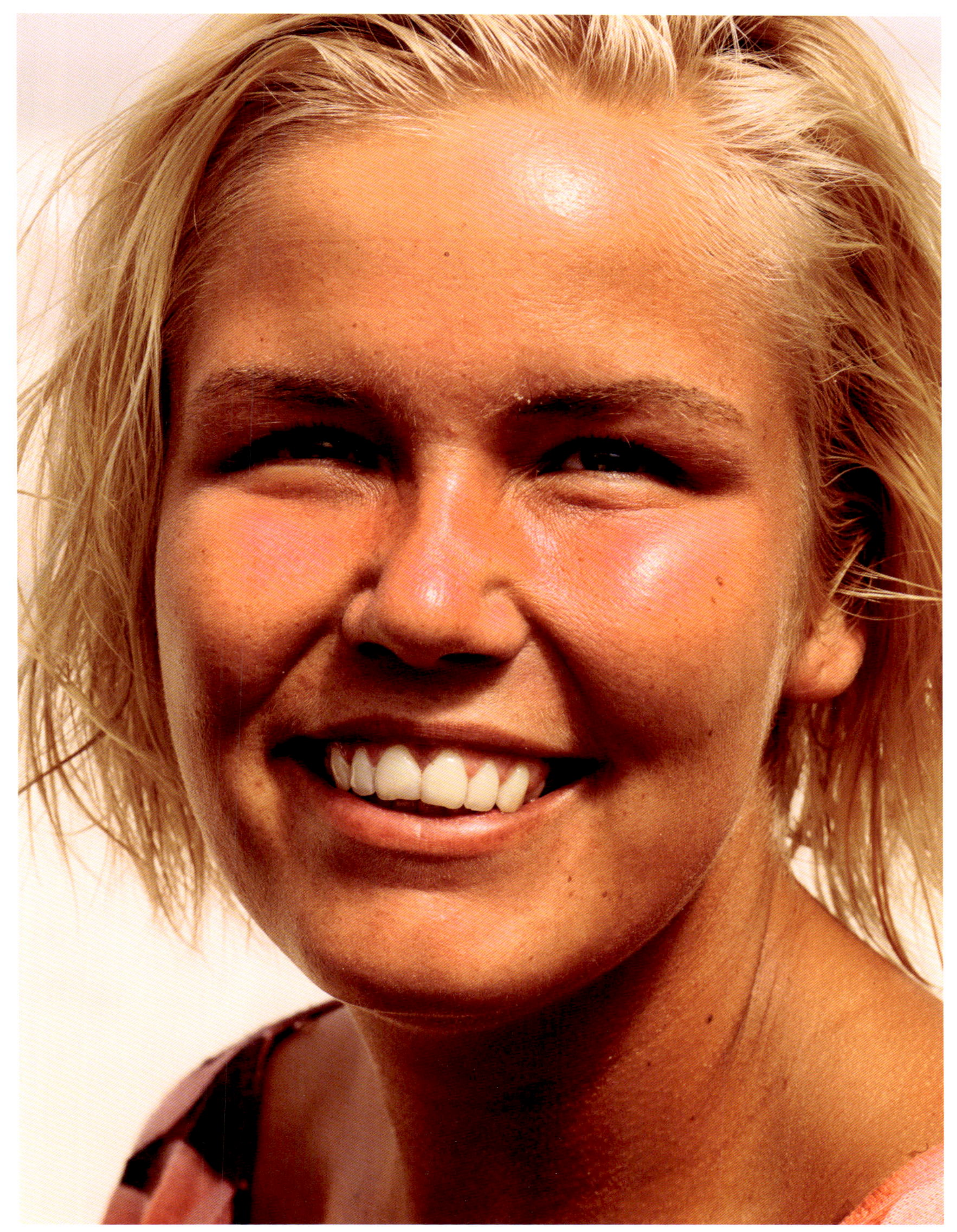

Lara. Coogee Beach

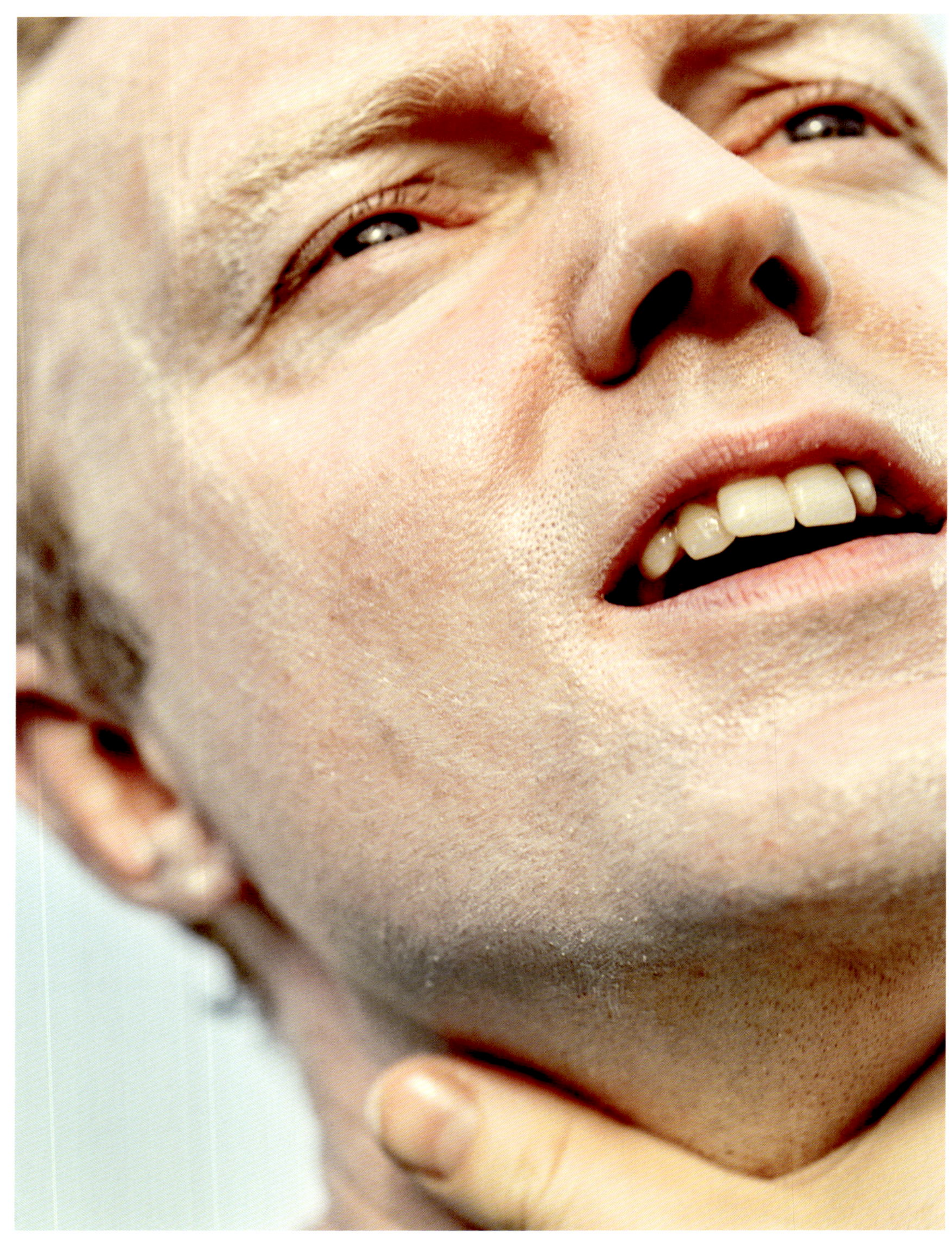

Sunscreen and Tom. Tamarama

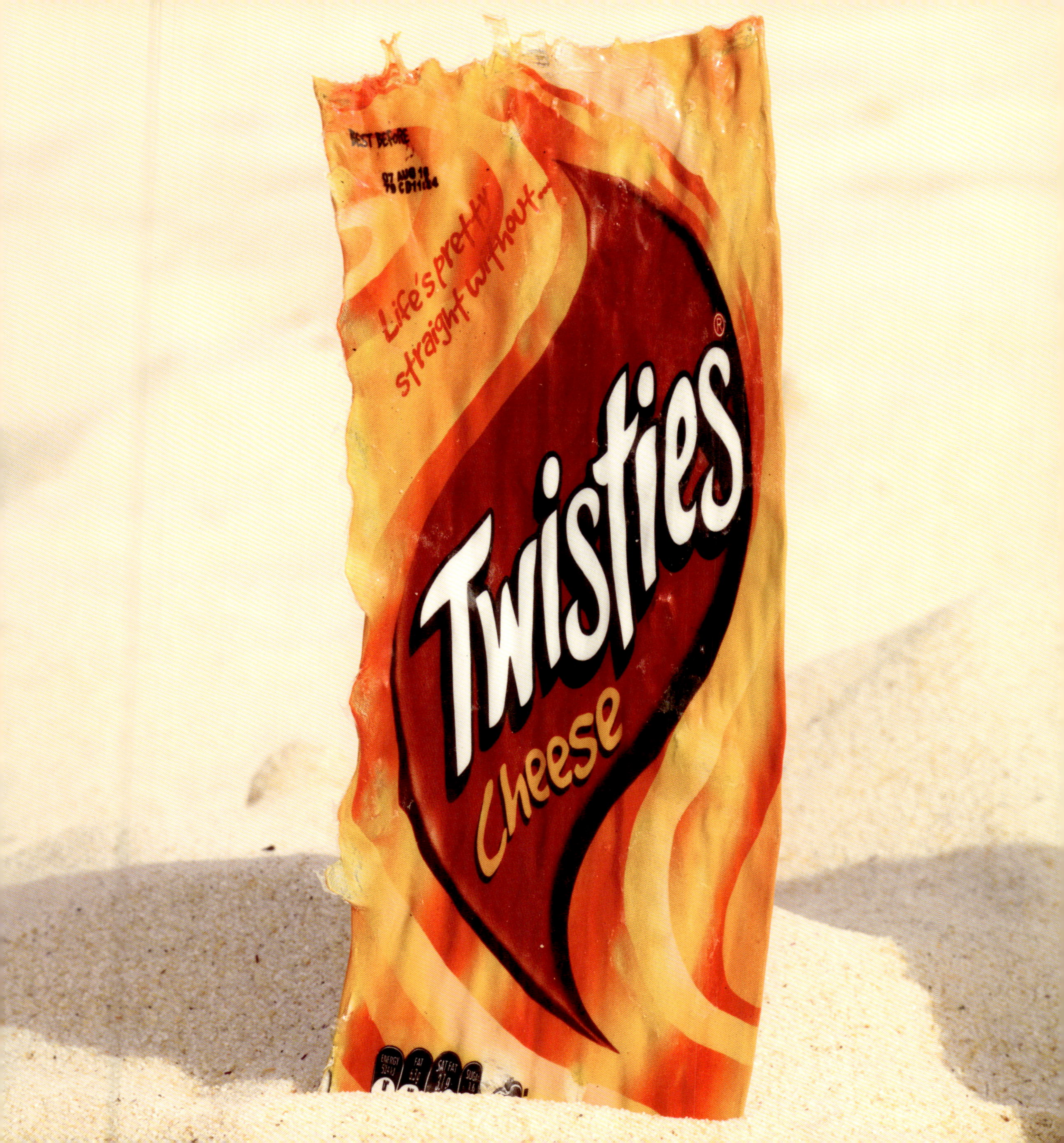

BEST BEFORE
Life's pretty straight without...
Twisties
Cheese

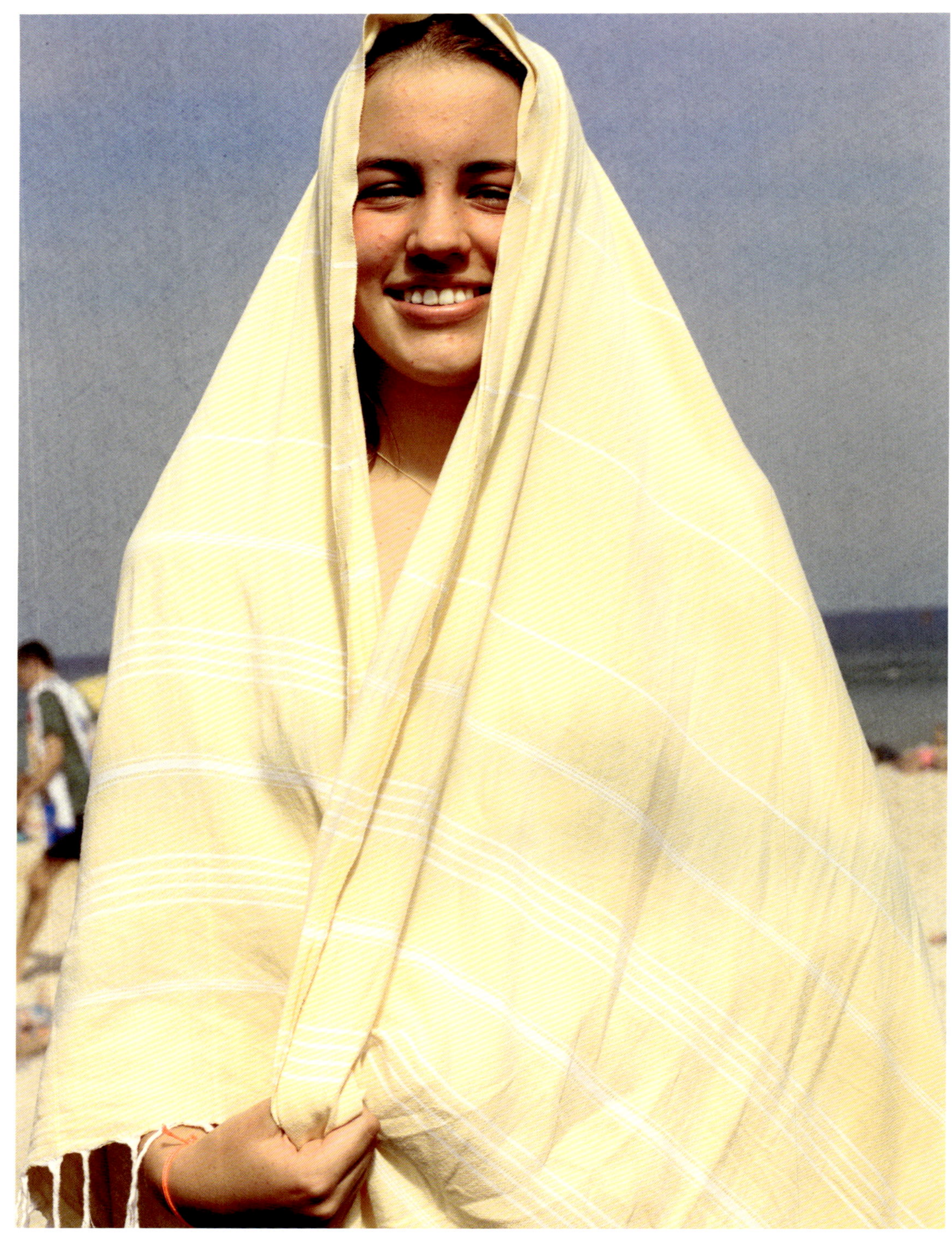

Mary. Bronte Beach

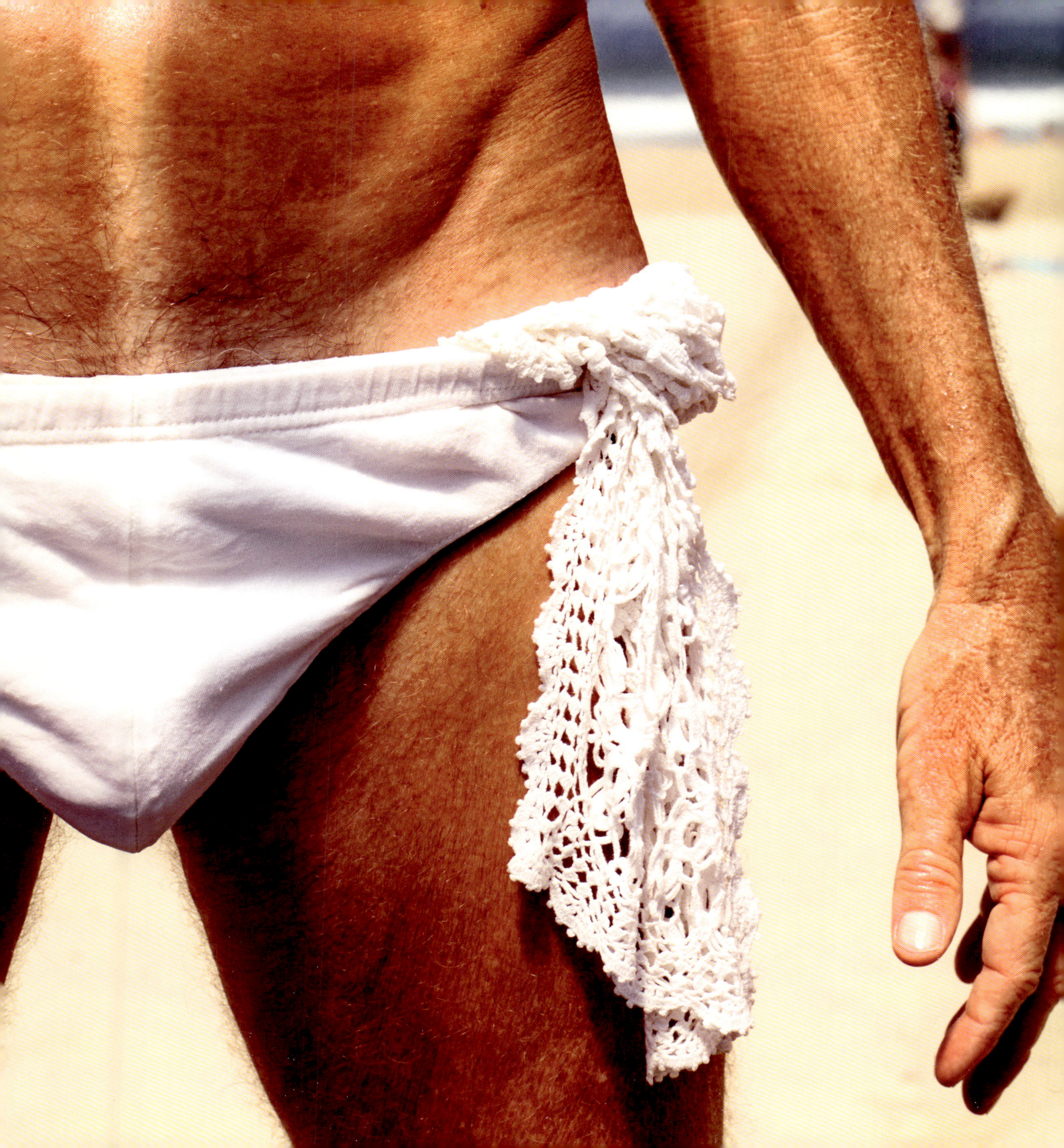

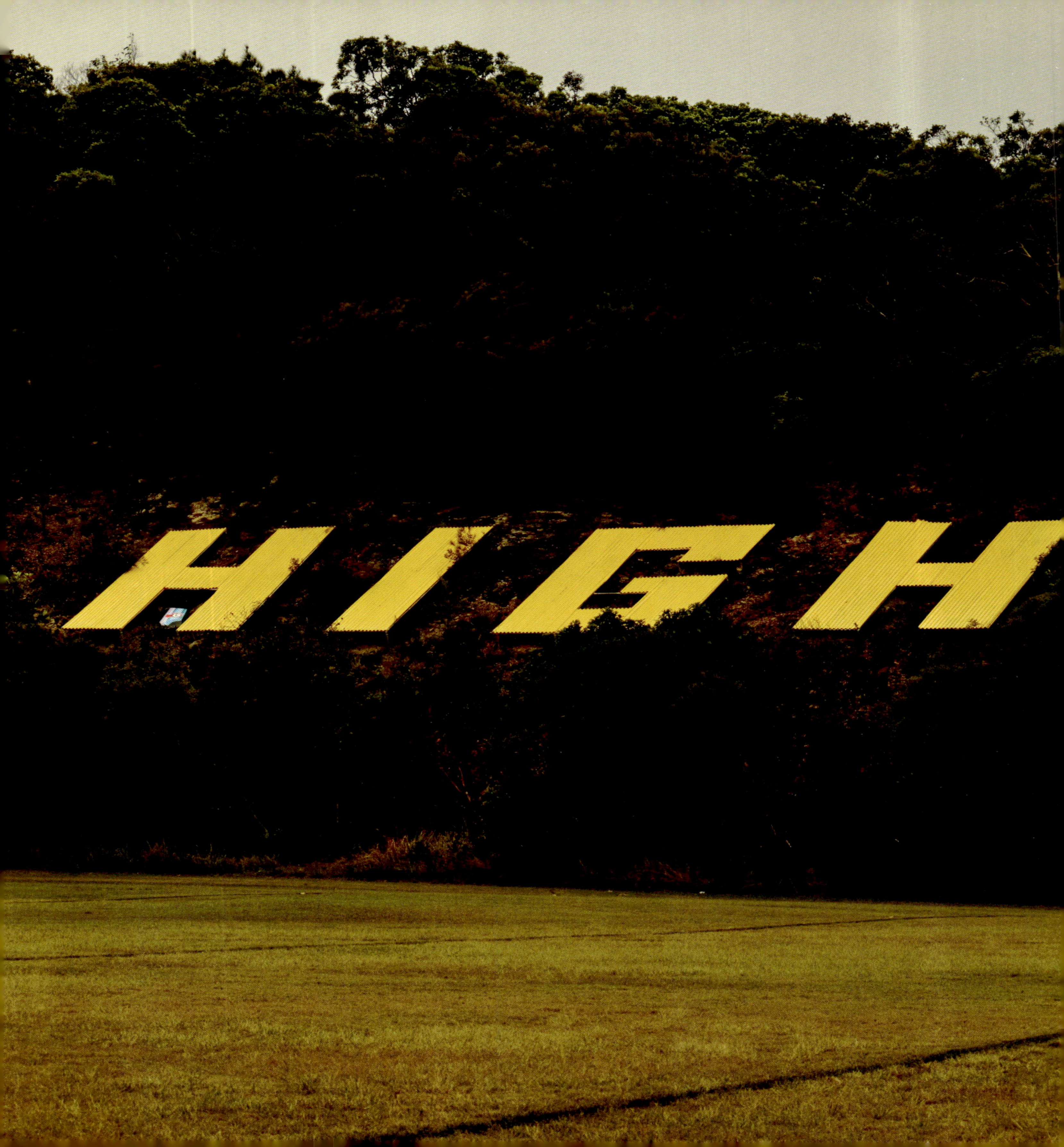
HIGH

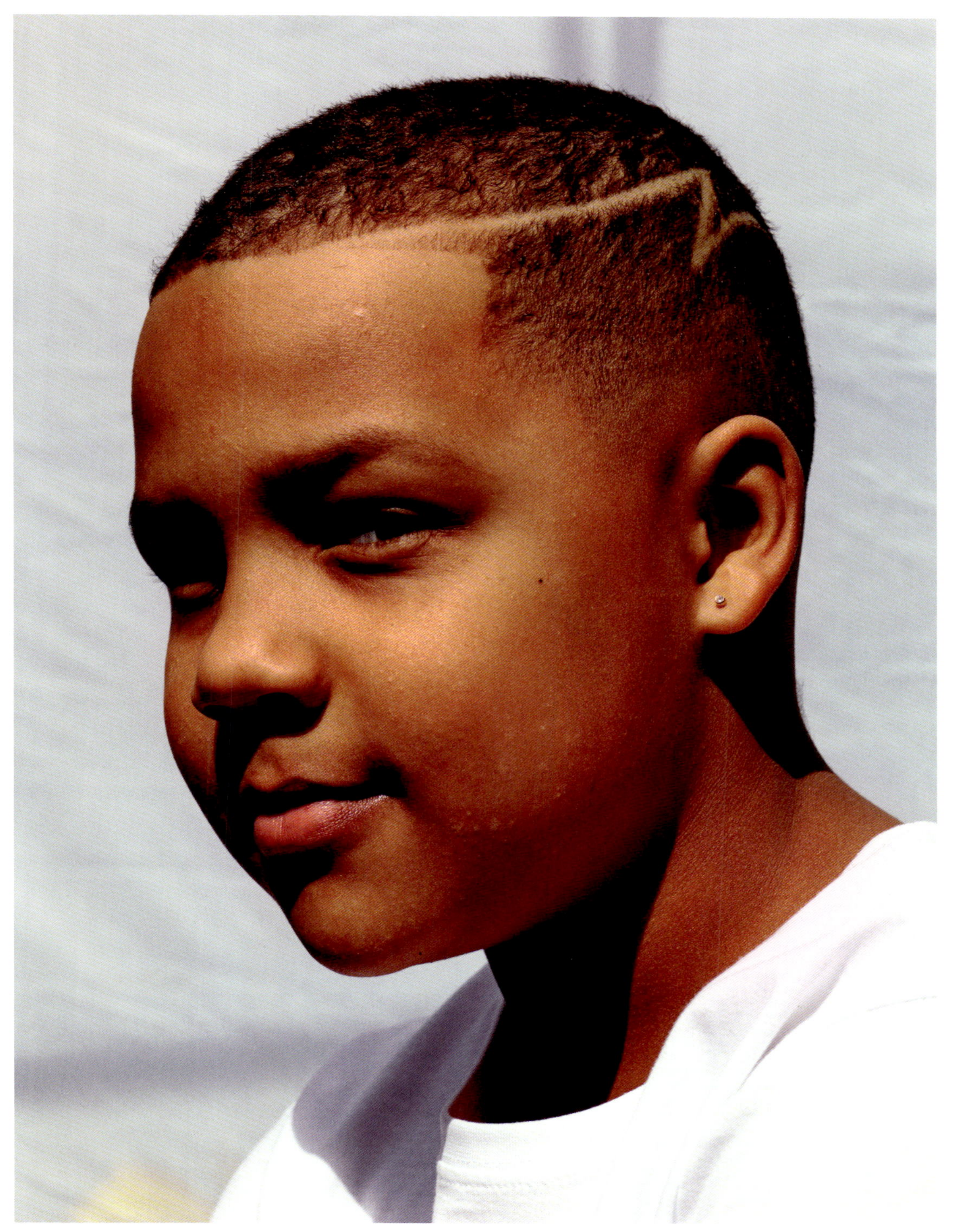

Alpha. Surfers Paradise

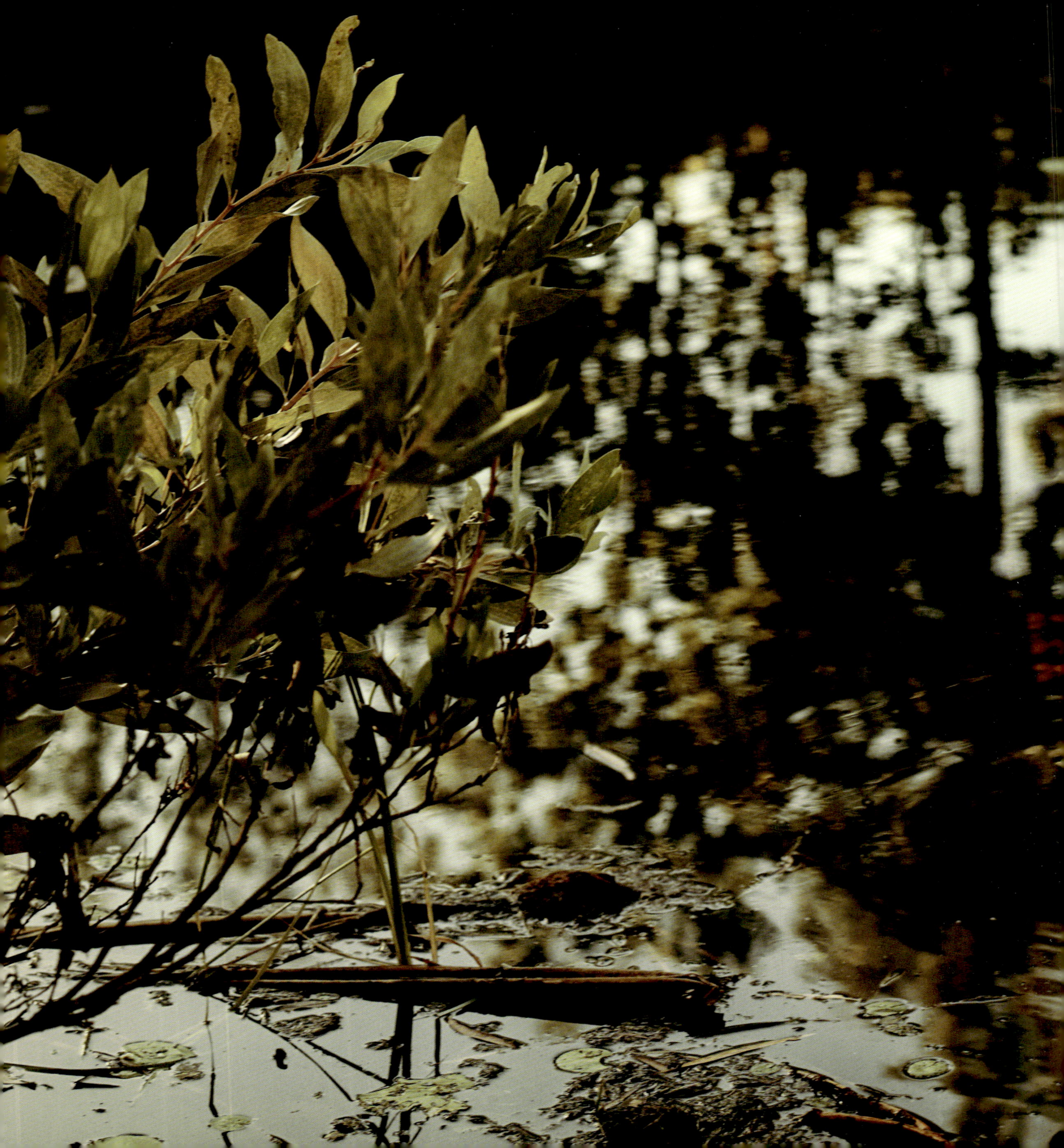

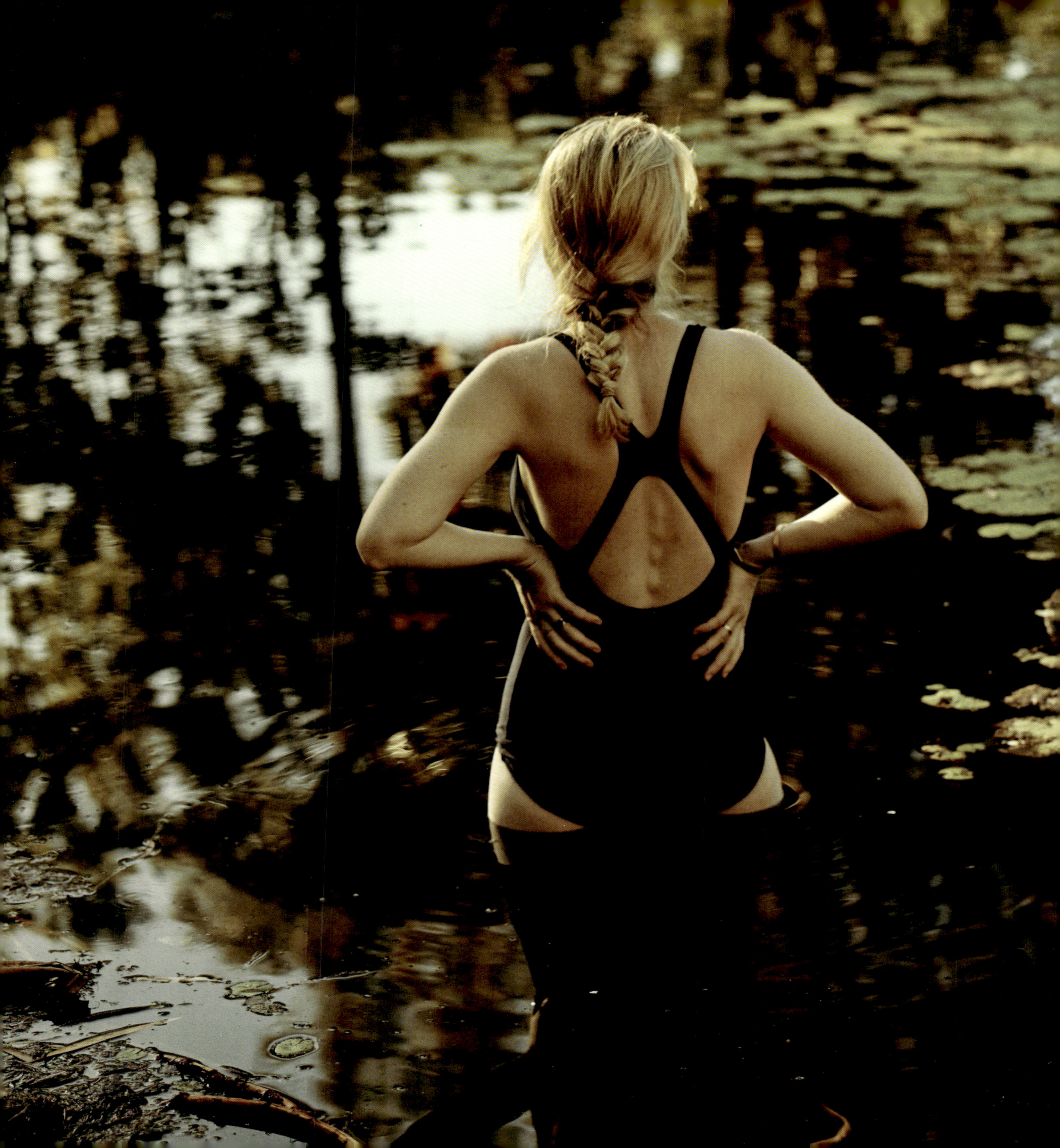

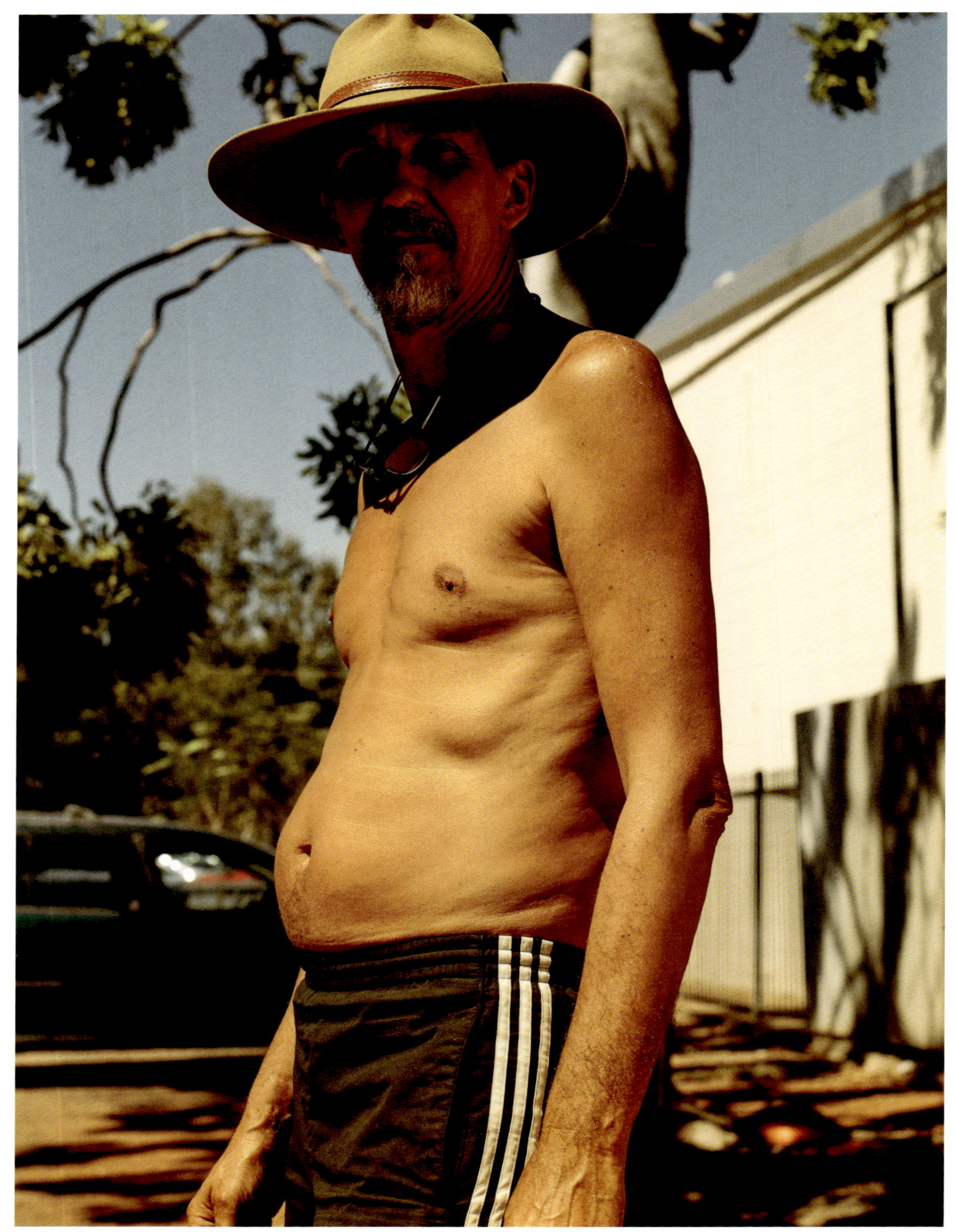

Mr. Roop. Wak Wak

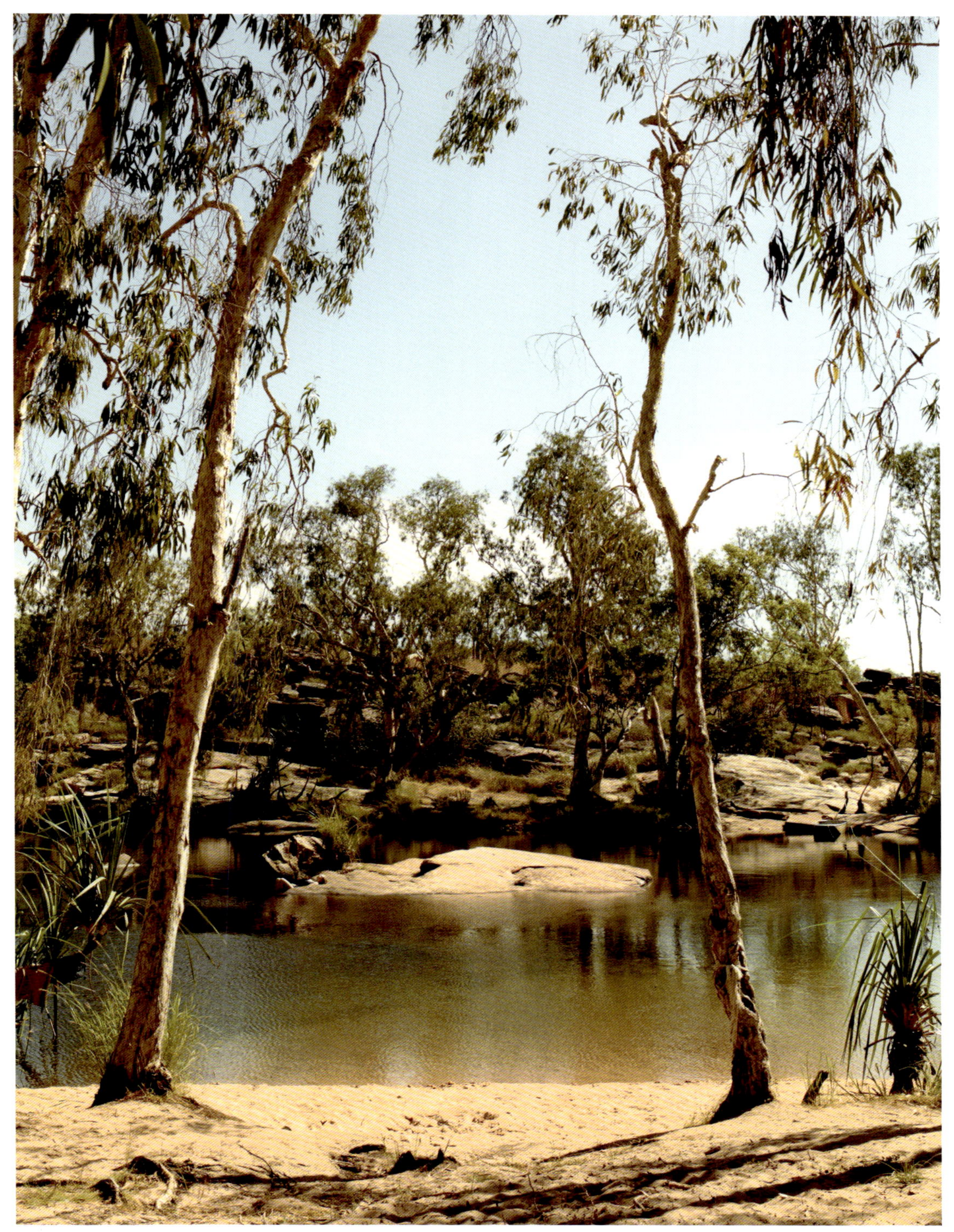

Paradise. Mount Barnett

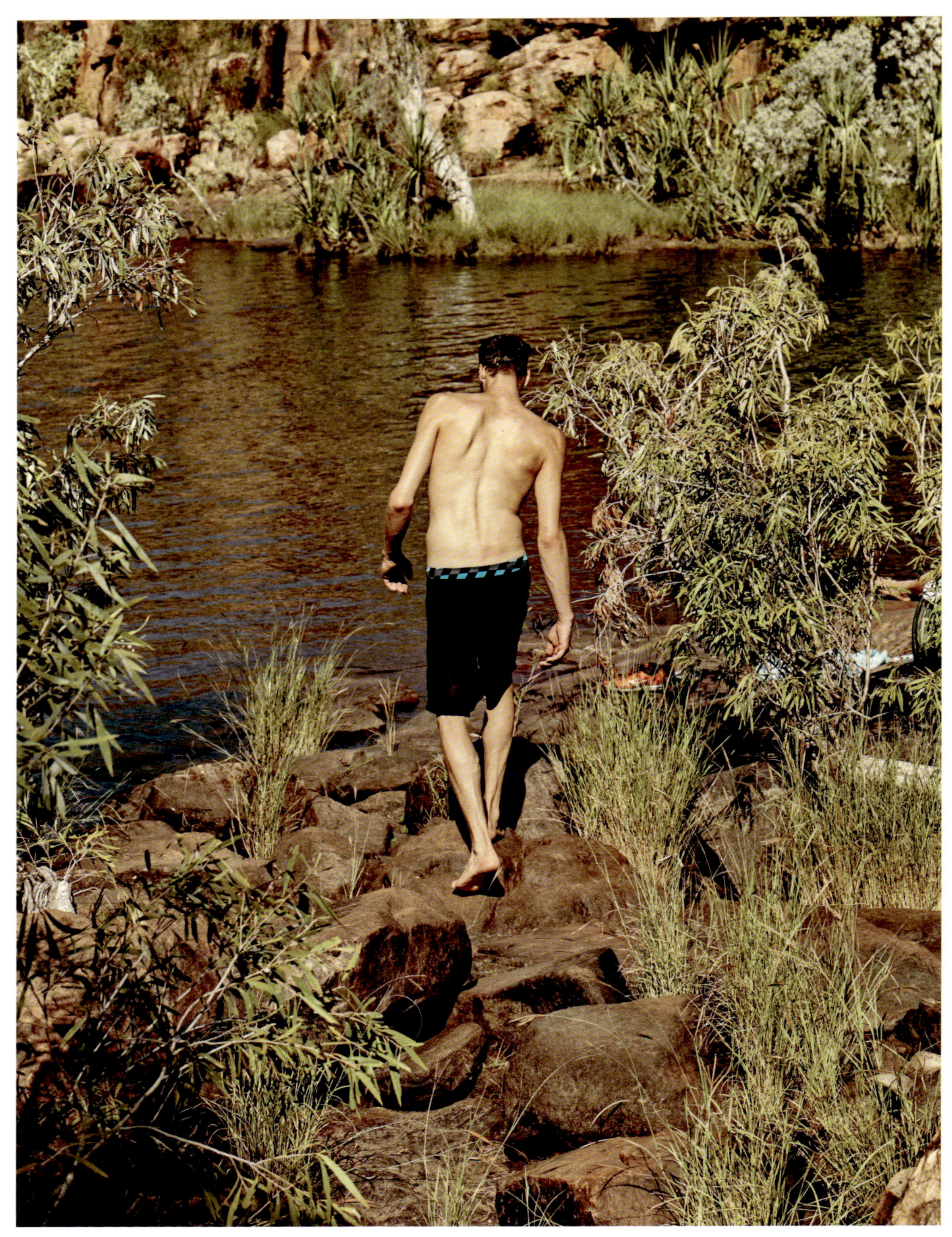

Spider. Emma's Gorge

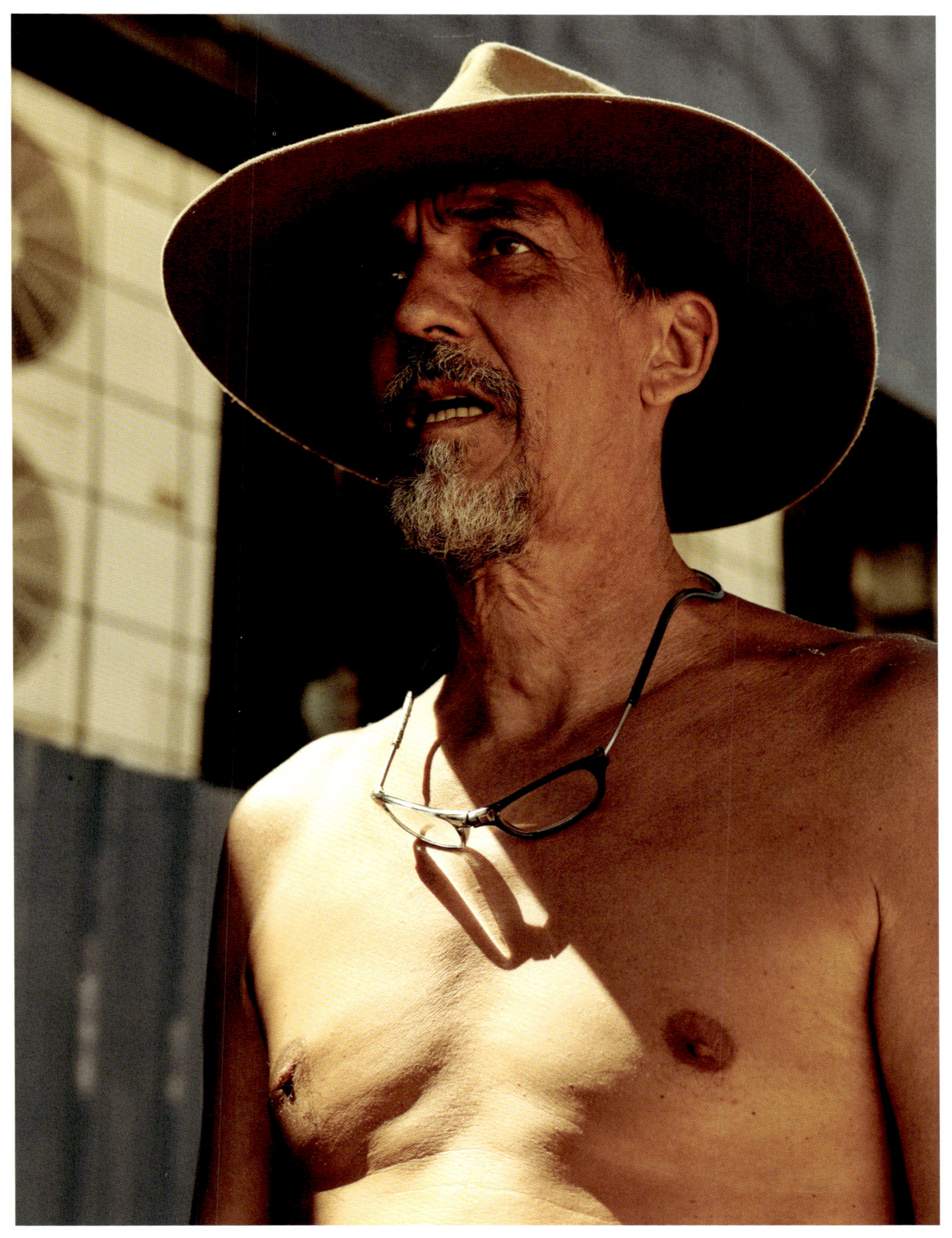

Mr. Roop. Wak Wak

NO
ENTRY

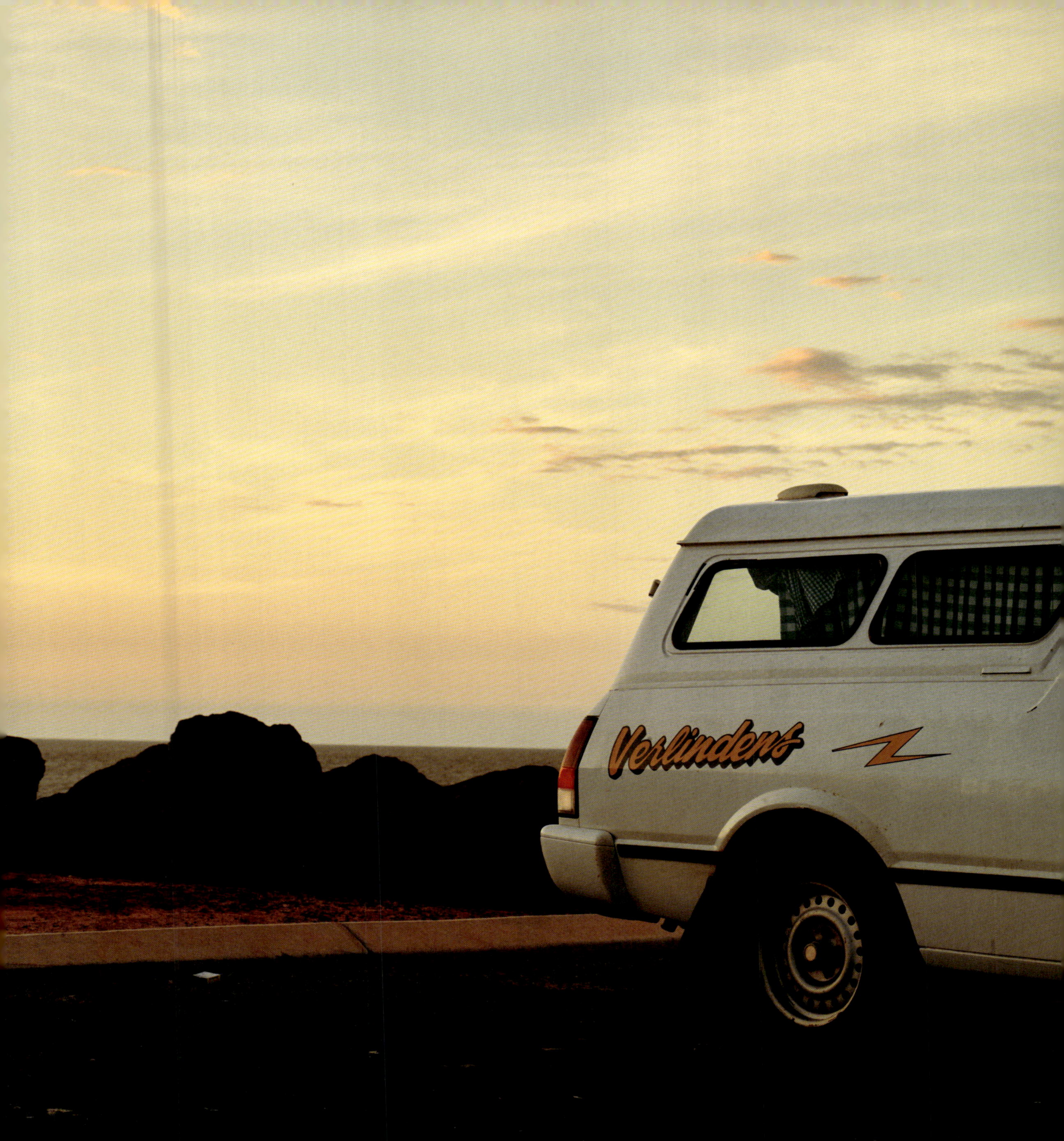
Verlindens

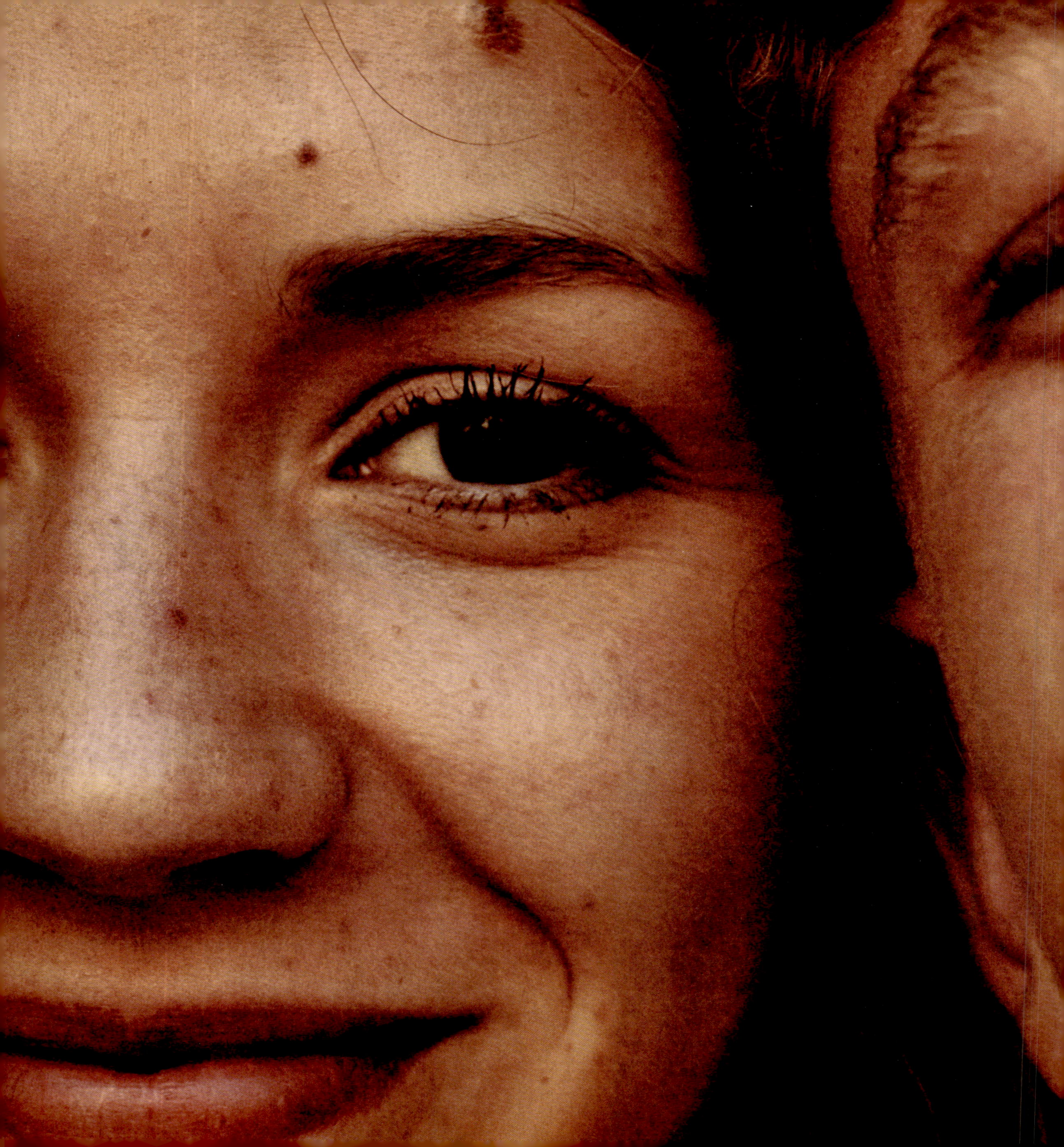

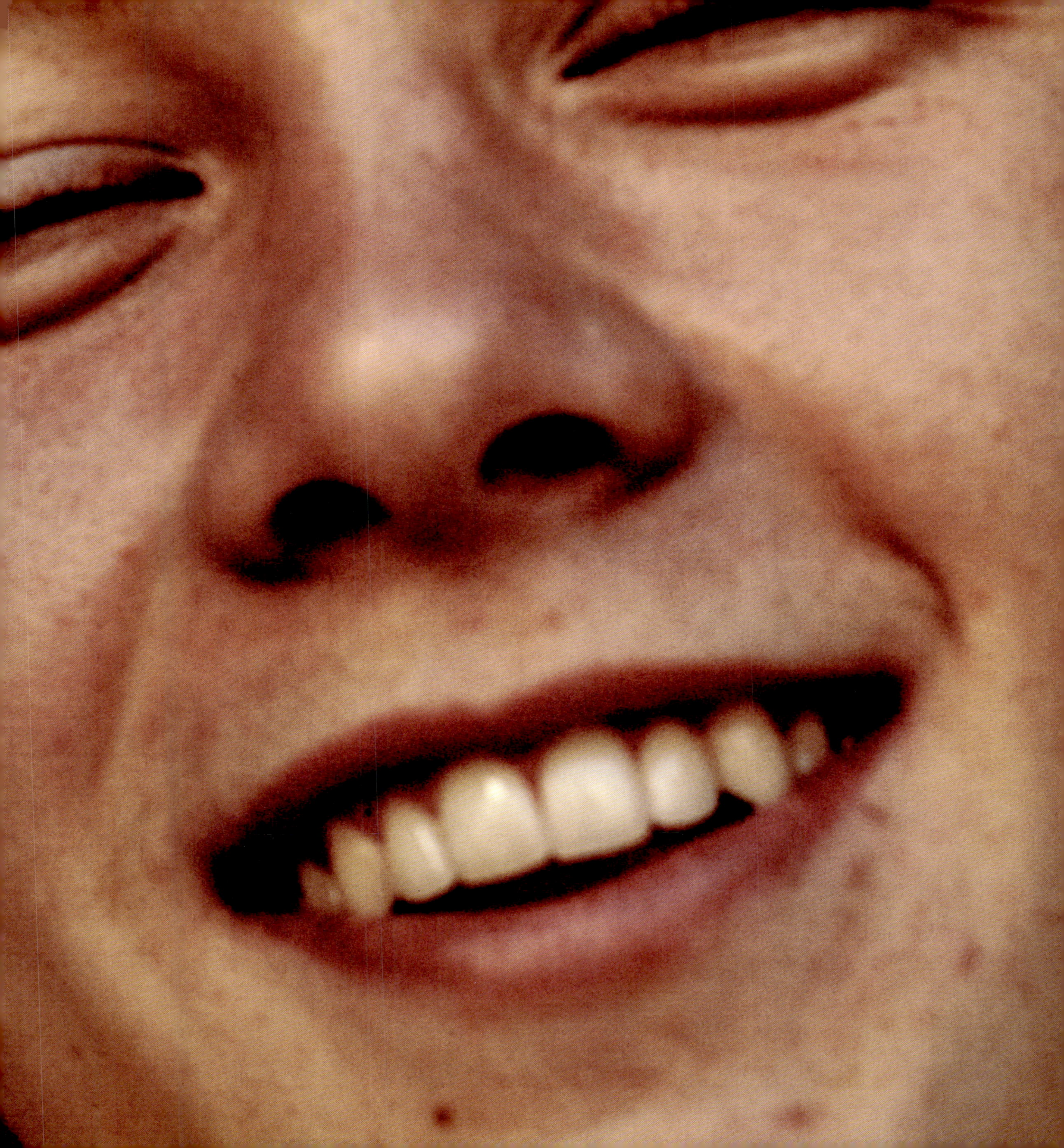

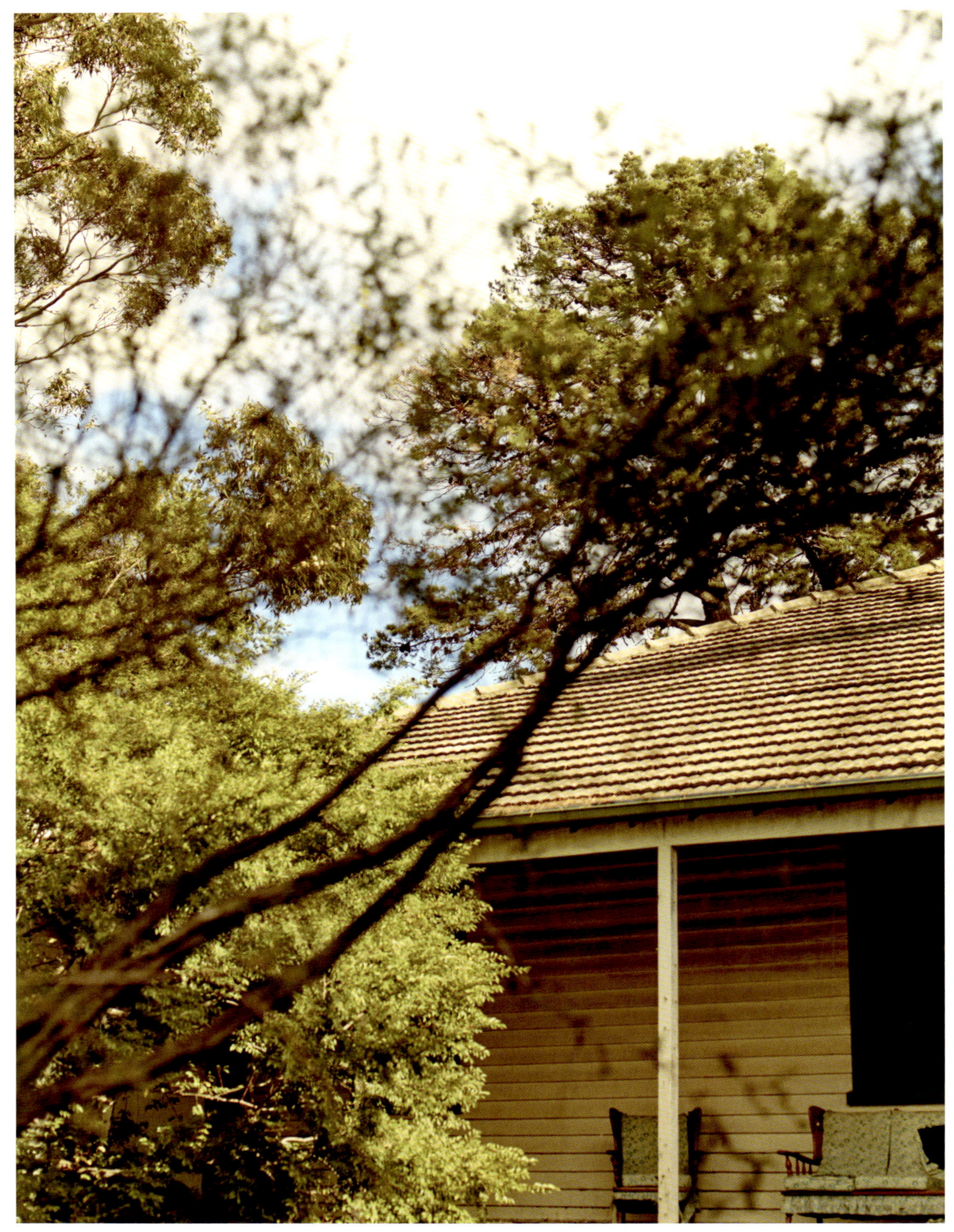

Pop's Porch. Longford

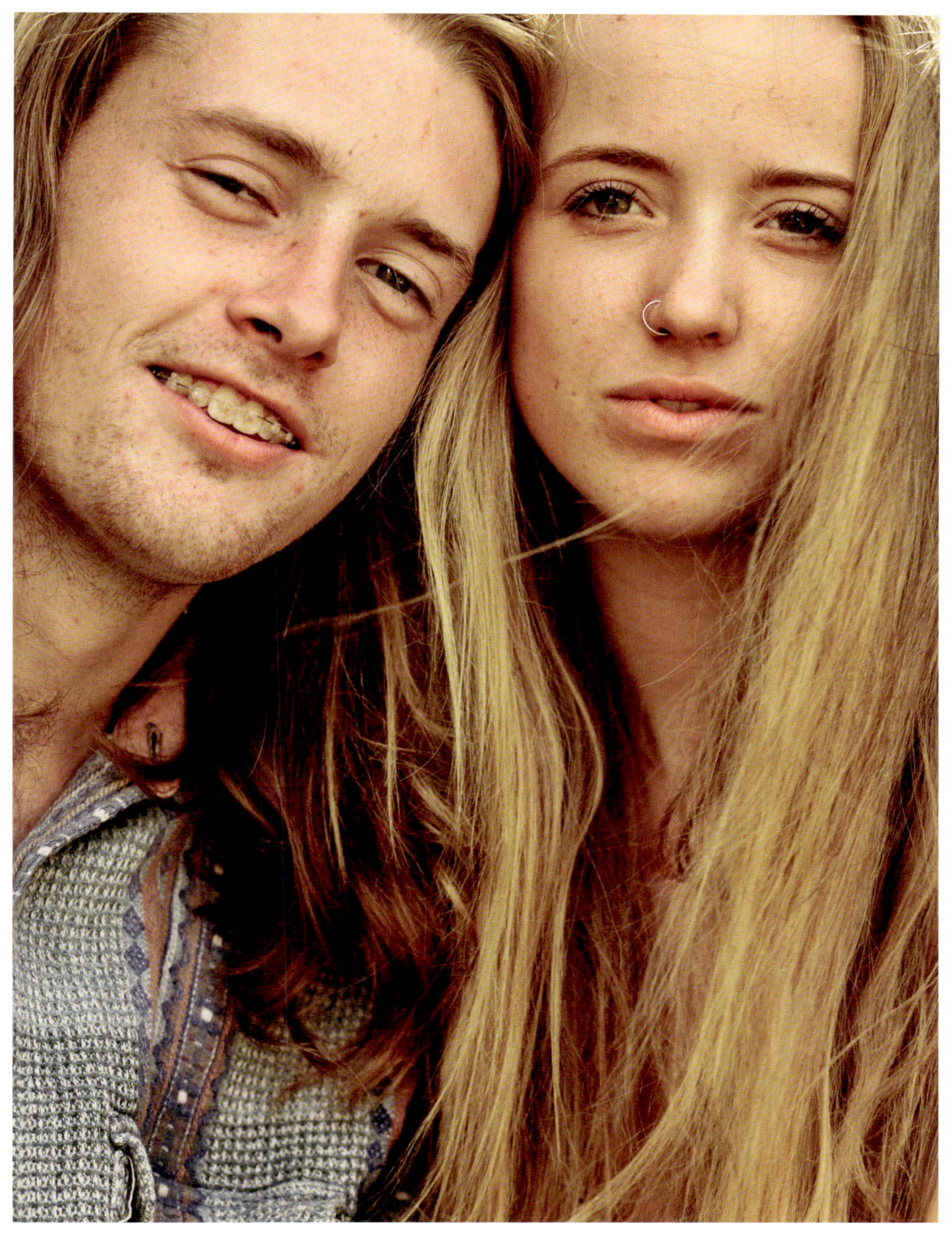

Willy and Sue. Sunday afternoon

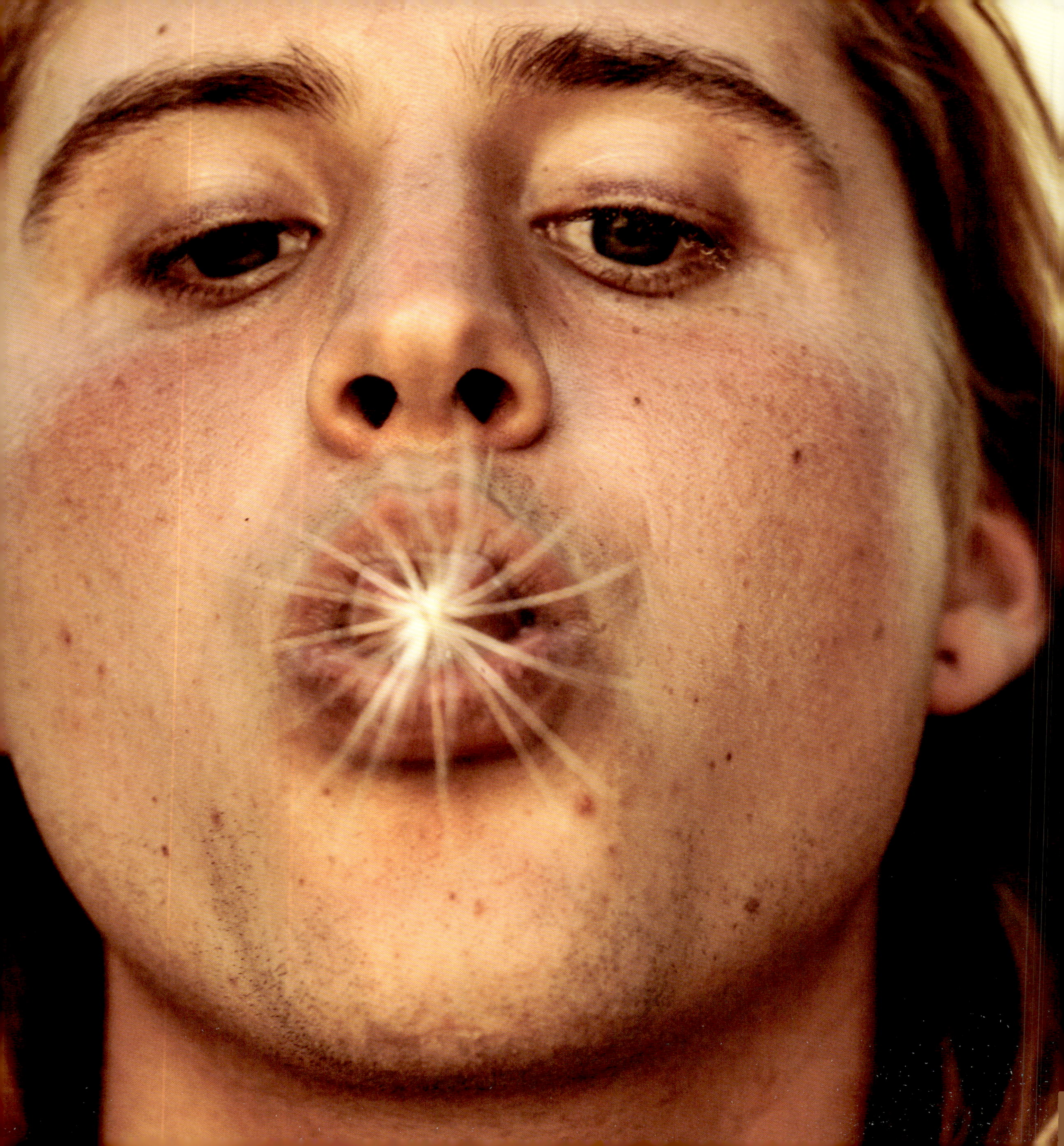

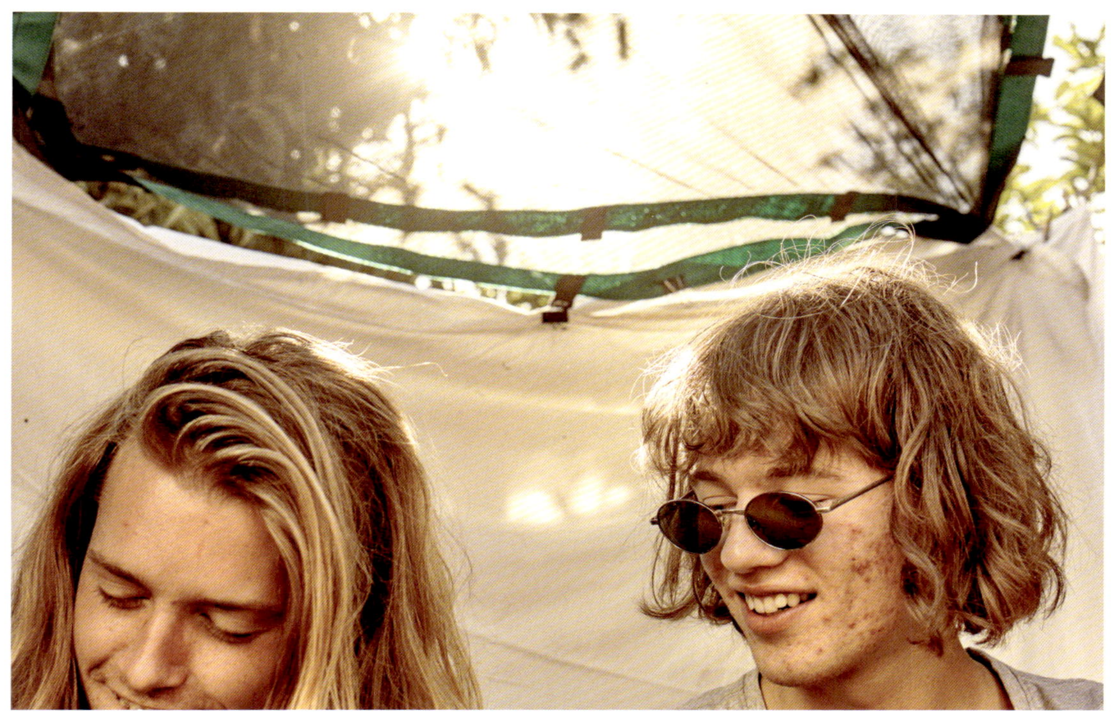

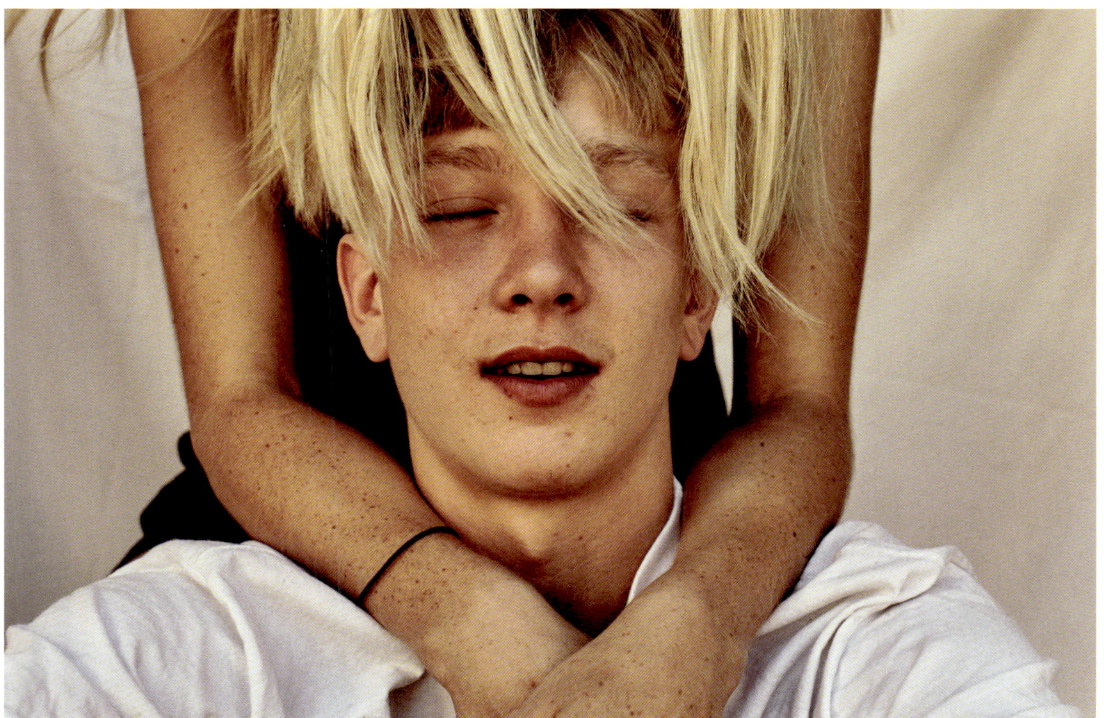

Sunday afternoon. Kyle and Pearl's Backyard

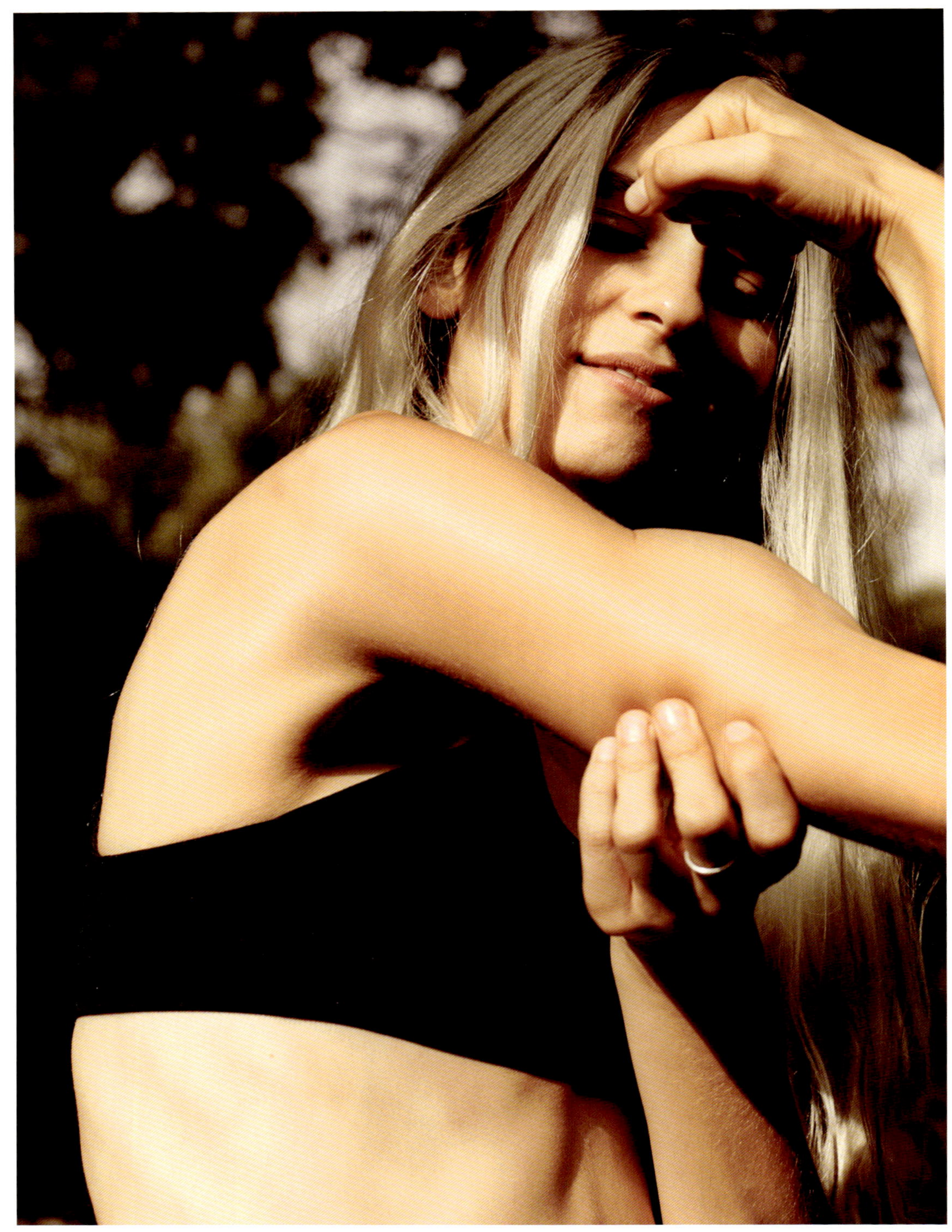

Banoffee. Brunswick

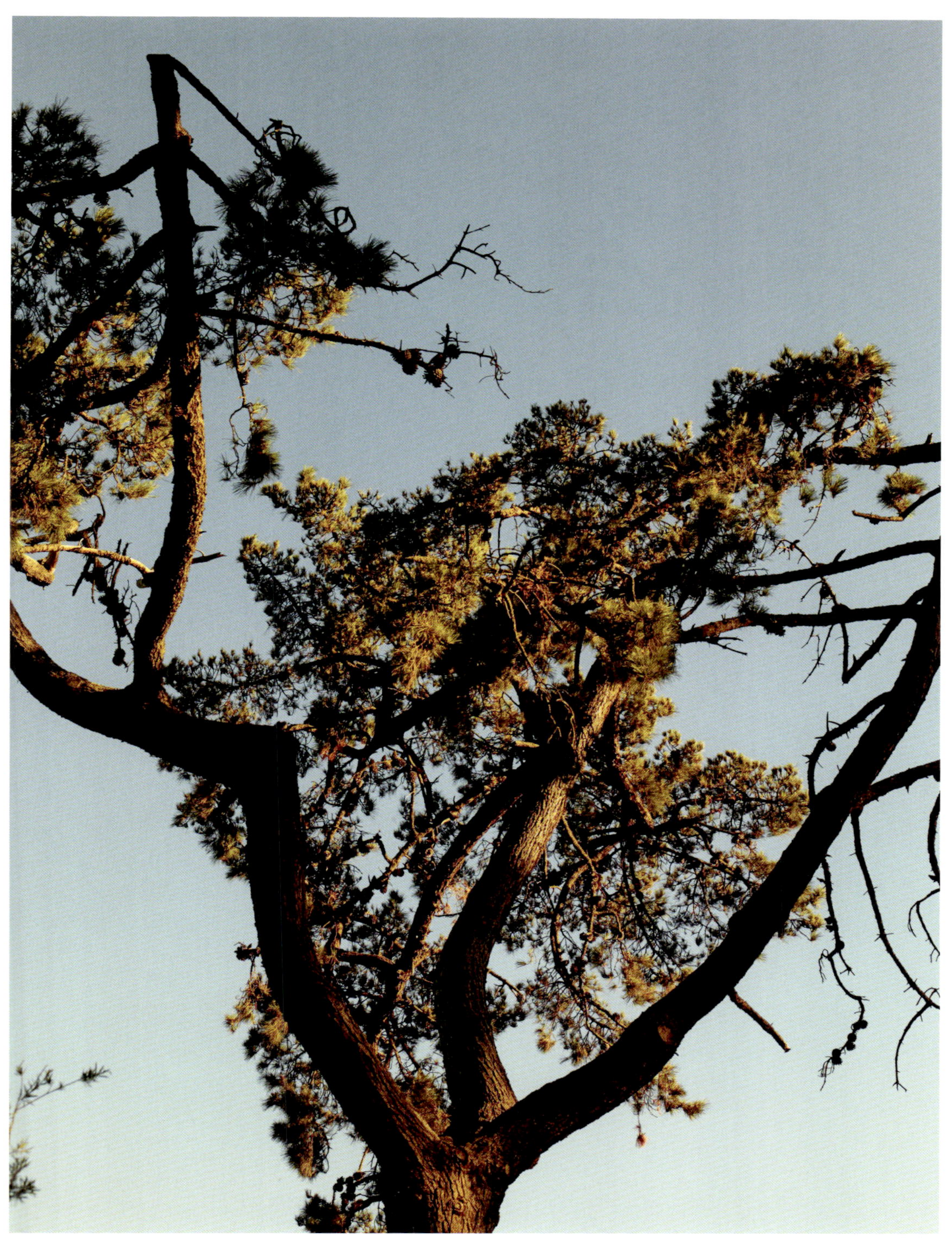

Sunrise. Ada's tree

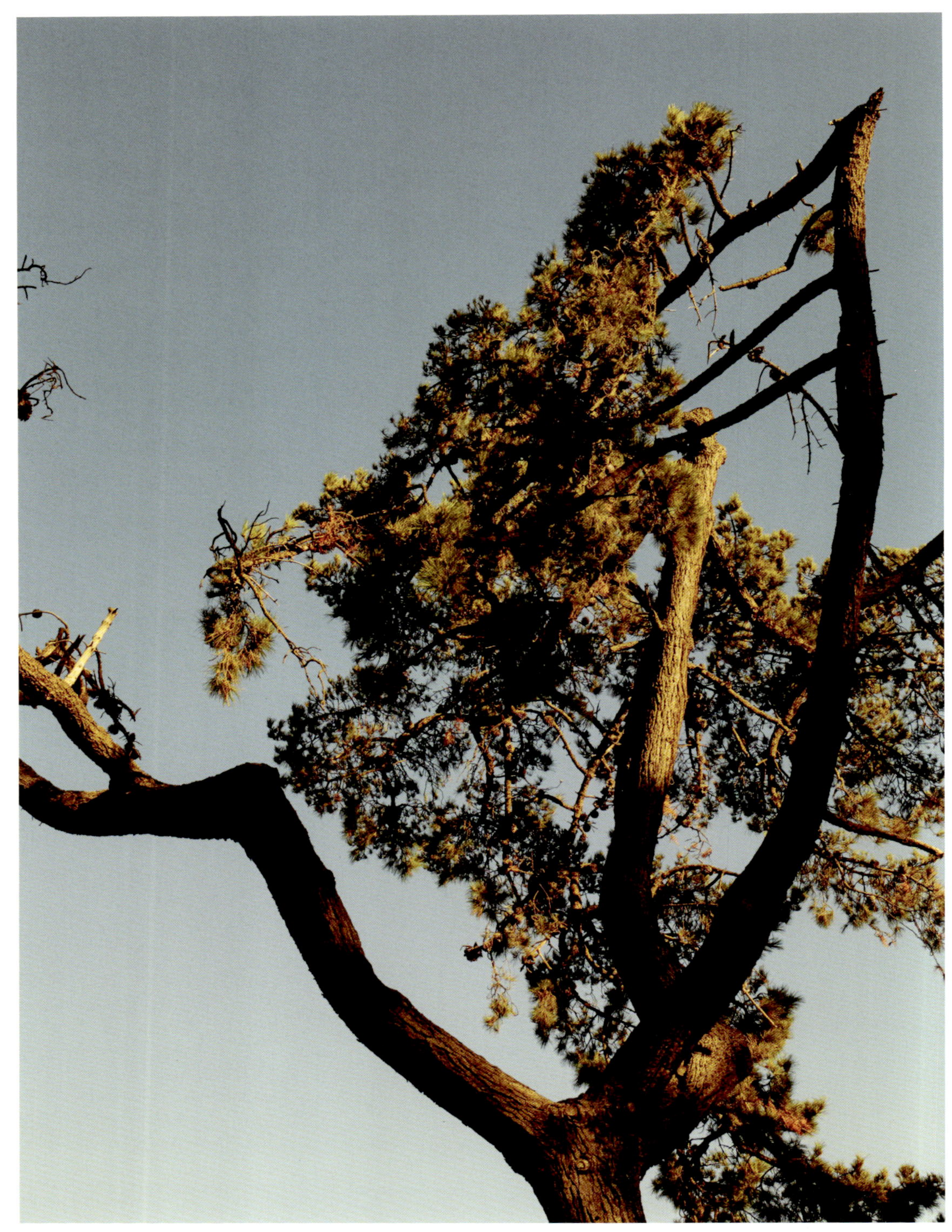

Sunset. Henry's Tree

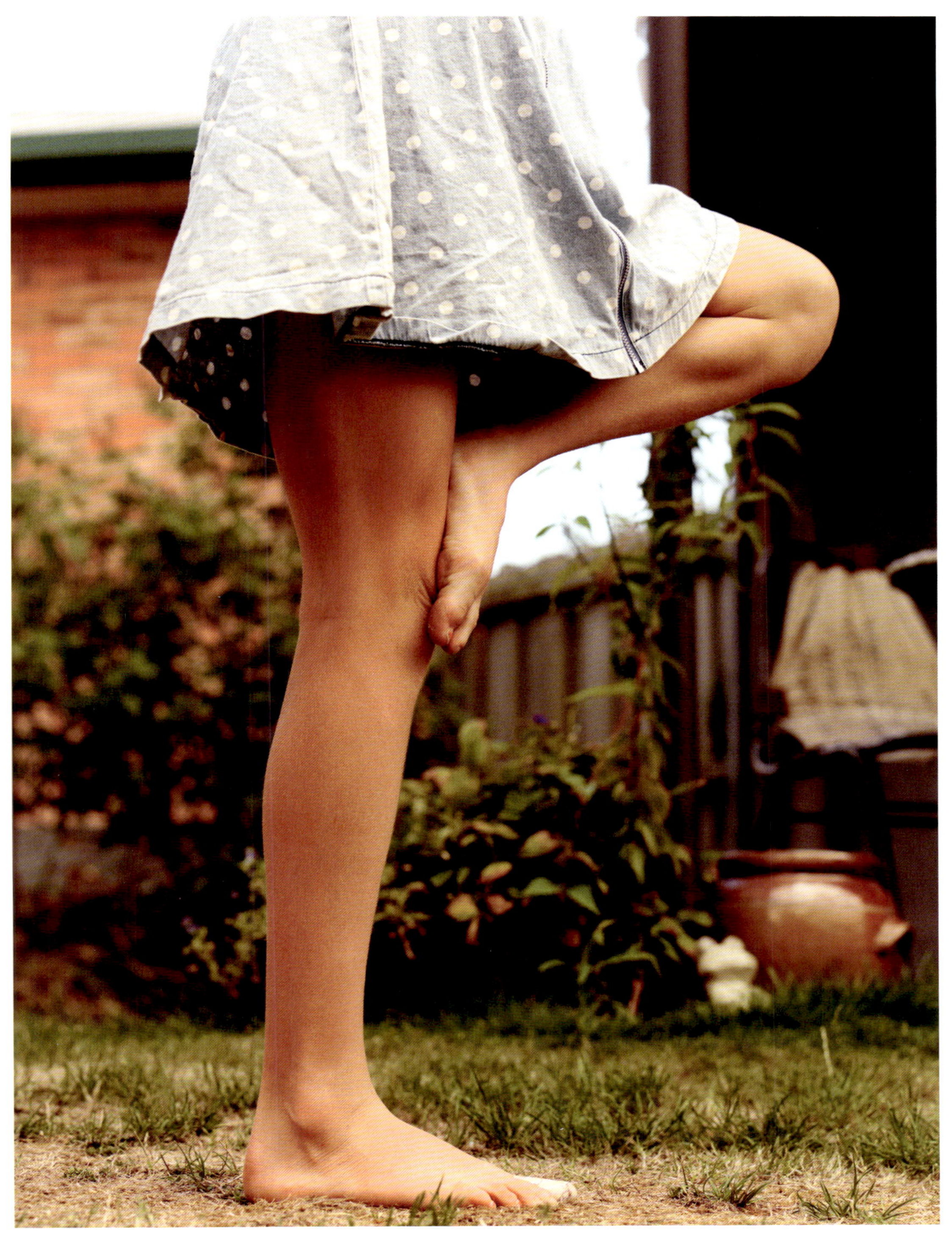

Chloe. Mum's backyard

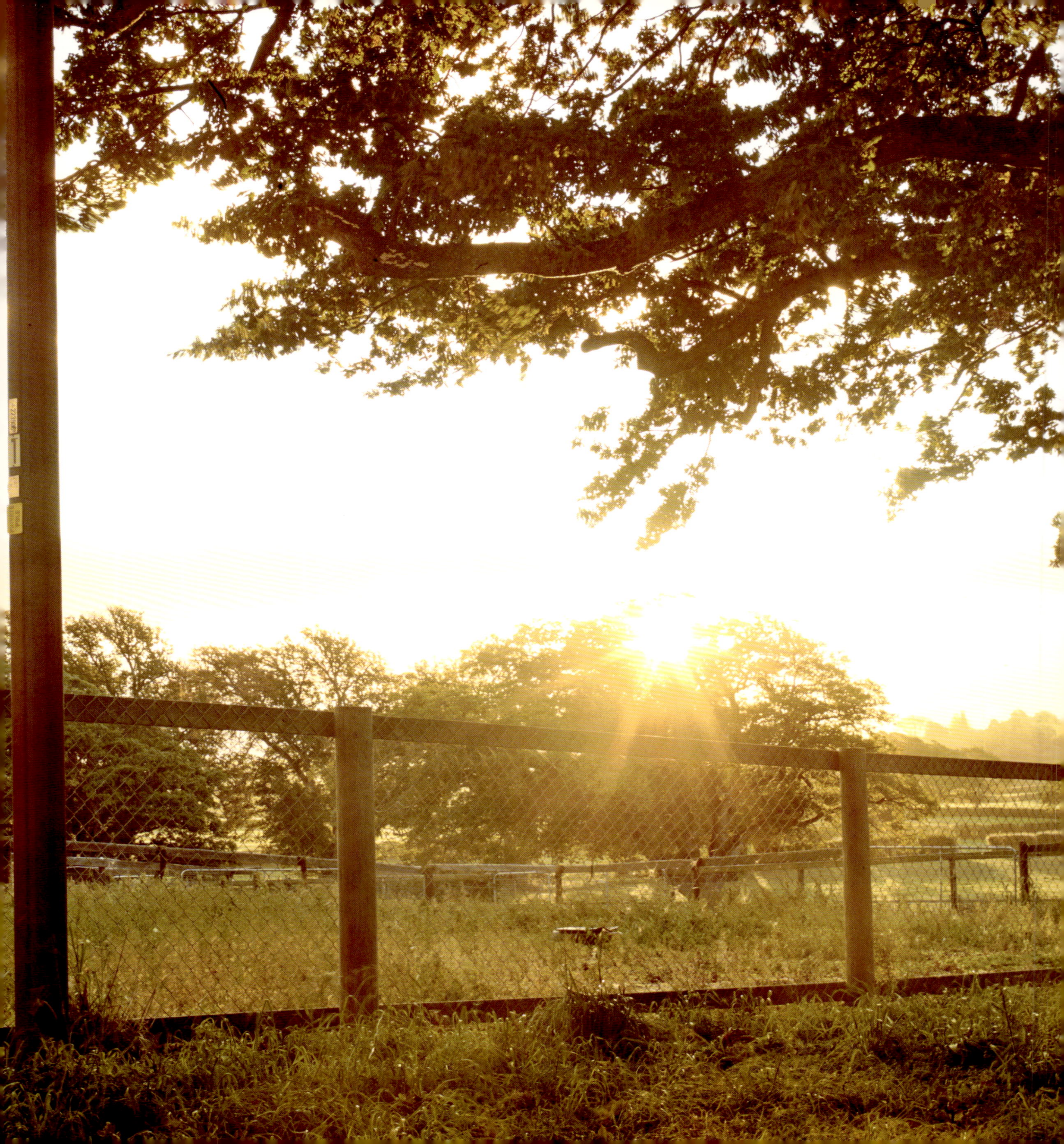

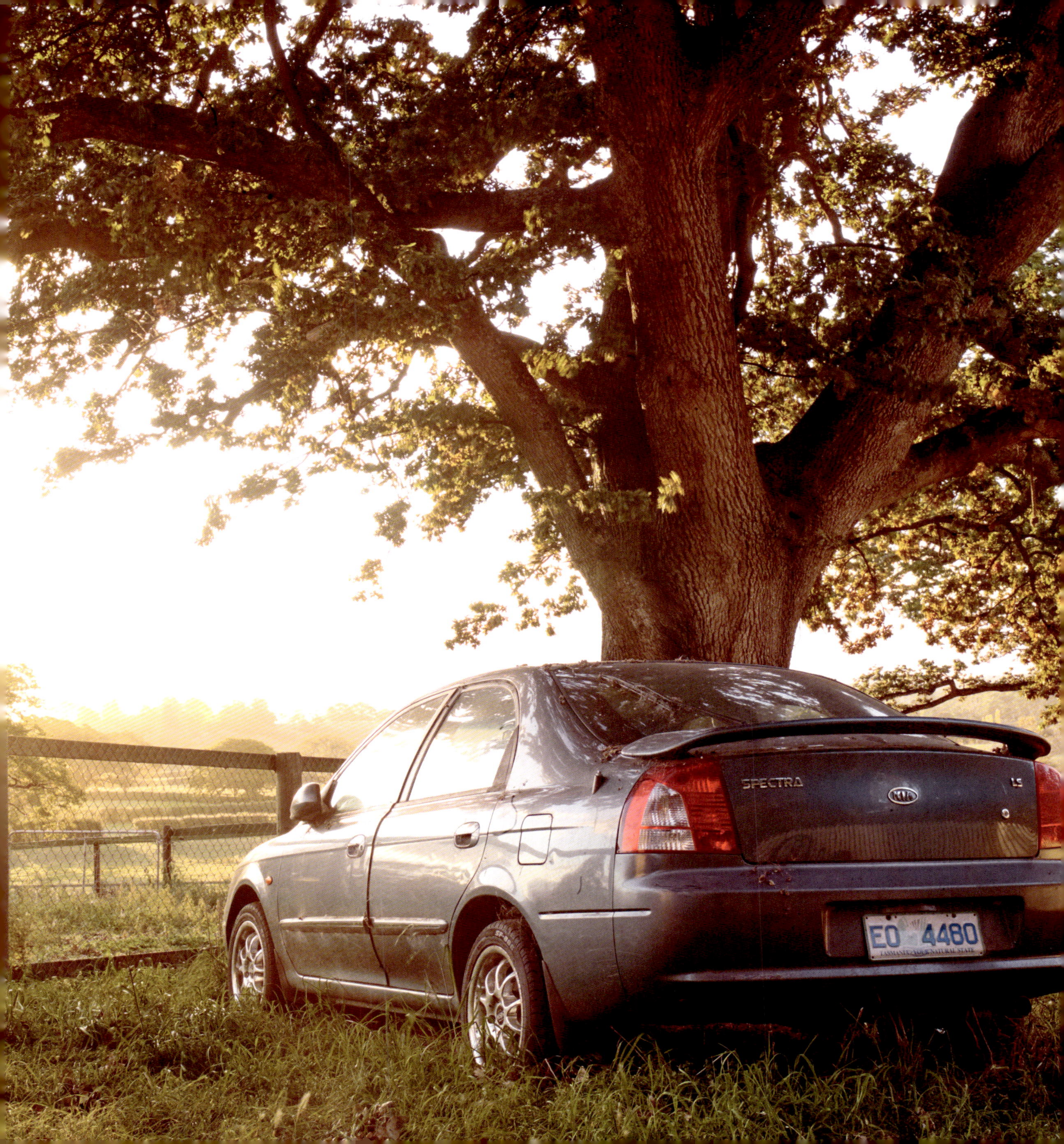

SPECTRA
KIA
LS
EO 4480

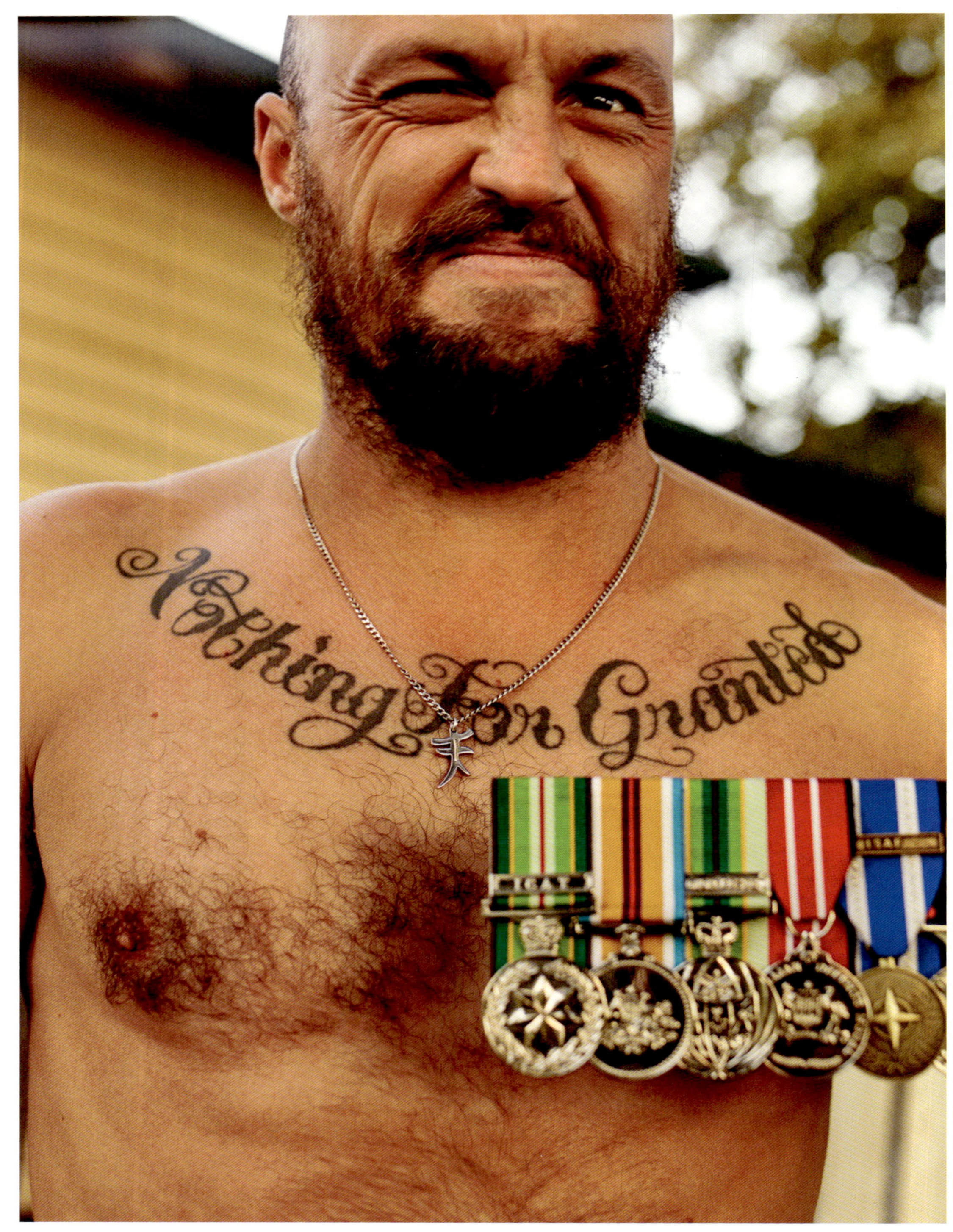

Nev. Poatina Road

AUSTRALIANA

BOOK DESIGN

Dean Langley

SPECIAL THANKS

Bradley Perkins, Rebeccah Mahne and Lara Blackwell-Sign for help on the ground
Jeanny Bachelin and Sebastien Servel and Dtouch NYC for color and contrast
Peter Disaster for the beer and backyard
Emily McCarron for everything else

PUBLISHED BY

Damiani srl

info@damianieditore.com
www.damianieditore.com

ISBN 978-88-6208-499-4

SIMON EELES

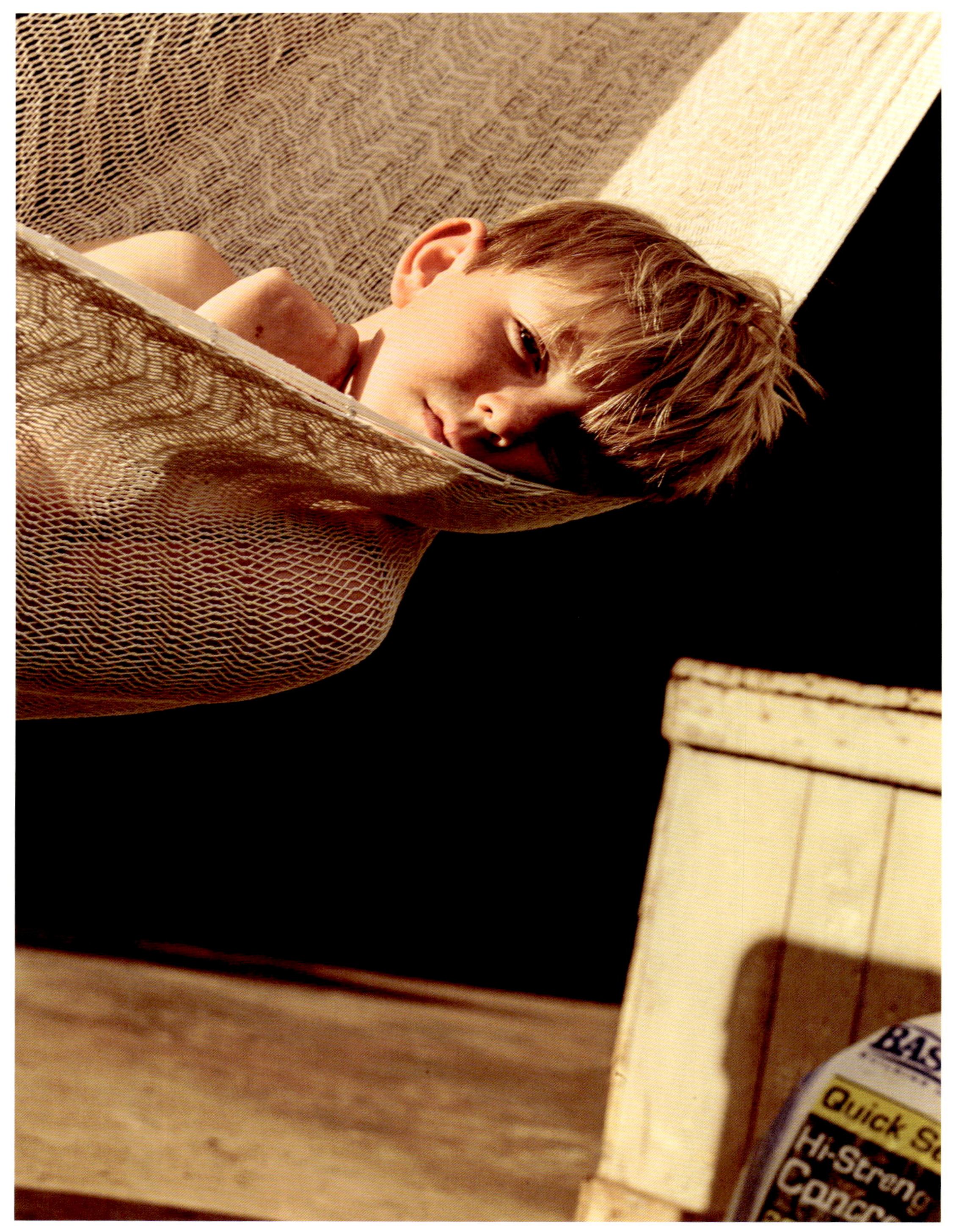

Jesse. Mum's backyard

THE END

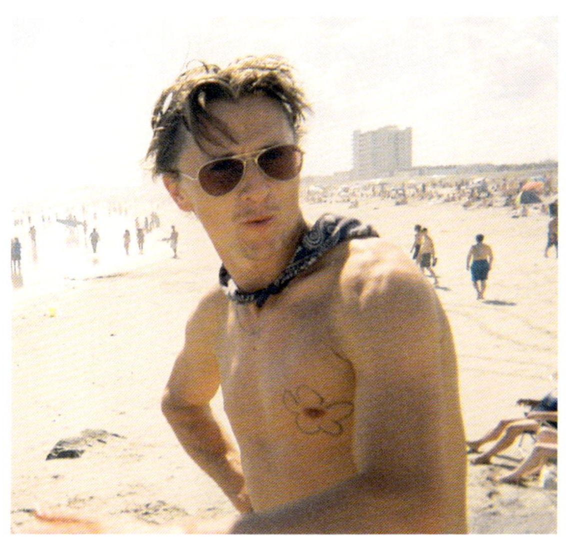

See you at the Rockaways…